"John Wijngaards is precisely the prophetic voice we need for our time as the Catholic Church wriggles out of its taut imperial chrysalis to fly at last on two wings, male and female, lay and ordained, equal in voice and decision-making, liberated from clericalism and legalism, free to love one another as Christ intended and as he loves us. If you want to know how to make that great transition, read this wonderful booklet and make the wisdom of these reflections your own!"

—MARY MCALEESE, president of Ireland (1997–2011)

"This book is an icebreaker in this crucial period of church reform. John Wijngaards the theologian puts his finger on keys issues for the church and offers new paths. Wijngaards the communicator addresses them in a refreshing way and makes his points in plain language. This is a book to savour and to help you promote a healthier church!"

—THOMAS O'LOUGHIN, director, Brepols Library of Christian Sources

"This is an incredibly engaging and creative work. John Wijngaards's lifetime of commitment to ministry in the church is brought to bear on the place of authority in the community of faith. The reflections that make up this fascinating book interweave personal experience and the practice of Jesus. They make for a thoroughly original account of the importance of personal discernment for a renewal in ecclesial vitality where it most importantly belongs, at the grassroots of church life."

—PAUL LAKELAND, director, Center for Catholic Studies, Fairfield University

"John Wijngaards's book is a timely collection of reflections proposing a Christocentric model of authority in the Church. Highly relevant in the light of Pope Francis's synodality, a journeying together through authentic dialogue, recognition, and embrace of the *sensus fidelium*, grounded in 'reality' and experiential learning. This learning invites all the faithful to reflect on authentic authority in the Church based in service, not power. I recommend this to individuals, faith groups, ˙   ˈ ˙ ˈ   ˙˙ ˙ "

—TODD SALZMAN, profess

D1378105

"This is a profoundly compassionate book drawing on John Wijngaards's vast ministerial experience. It is a wonderful collection of practical meditations that will help adult Christians reflect on their experience. The book shifts our attention away from superficial piety toward a deeper understanding of faith that is focused on Jesus and the Gospels. It's a book for daily reflection that fills the void that many people of faith are experiencing as our church moves from outdated religiosity to a practice of faith relevant to our world and future generations."

—PAUL COLLINS, author of *Papal Power*

"Multiple cracks in the Church's structures open it to a reality check. John Wijngaards challenges clerical power with Christ's inclusive authority. Replete with humor, true story, and exegesis, the reader is invited to reflect upon how the Church is to organize itself. A timely work. These daily meditations grapple with existential questions that open us to a Church finally moving forward."

—JANE ANDERSON, adjunct research fellow, University of Western Australia

"John Wijngaards has produced an eye-opening and thought-provoking book of concise daily reflections designed to be read and digested over the course of a month. Each one begins with Scripture, an amusing cartoon, and a personal story or anecdote from Wijngaards's life experience around the world. The theological unfolding that follows is entirely digestible and accessible, not intimidating, the conclusions logical and common sense. These reflections can be used with profit by anyone."

—SUSAN K. ROLL, professor emerita of feminist theology, University of Ottawa

Christ's Idea of Authority
in the Church

Christ's Idea of Authority in the Church

Reflections on Reform

JOHN WIJNGAARDS

WIPF *&* STOCK · Eugene, Oregon

CHRIST'S IDEA OF AUTHORITY IN THE CHURCH
Reflections on Reform

Copyright © 2023 John Wijngaards. All rights reserved. Except for brief quotations in critical publications or reviews, no part of this book may be reproduced in any manner without prior written permission from the publisher. Write: Permissions, Wipf and Stock Publishers, 199 W. 8th Ave., Suite 3, Eugene, OR 97401.

Wipf & Stock
An Imprint of Wipf and Stock Publishers
199 W. 8th Ave., Suite 3
Eugene, OR 97401

www.wipfandstock.com

PAPERBACK ISBN: 978-1-6667-8796-2
HARDCOVER ISBN: 978-1-6667-8797-9
EBOOK ISBN: 978-1-6667-8798-6

08/18/23

Painting on cover by Jackie Clackson. ©wijngaardsinstitute

Comic drawings by Tom Adcock. ©wijngaardsinstitute

Scripture quotations from New International Version

Contents

Introduction		ix
1	Power? Yes, but . . .	1
2	Power to spread God's Kingdom	5
3	Power of the keys	9
4	Power to bind or to loosen	13
5	Power to forgive sins	17
6	Power to save lives	20
7	Power to drive out mental demons	24
8	Power to liberate	28
9	The authority of women	33
10	The authority of teachers	38
11	The authority of prophets	42
12	The authority of the community	47
13	The authority of the Catholic 'sense of faith'	52
14	Latent spiritual authority shared by all	57
15	No superior dignity	62
16	No immunity from secular law	67
17	Not office bound	72
18	Not of this world!	77
19	No ministry to enjoy luxury	81
20	No institutional control without accountability	85
21	No small-talk sermons	91
22	Authority reform—ministry in times to come	96

CONTENTS

23 Authority reform—women deacons   100

24 Authority Reform—talk to opponents   105

25 Authority Reform—step by step   110

26 Authority Reform—allow more regional variation   115

27 Authority Reform—can a schism be avoided?   120

28 Authority Reform—it will happen!   124

    Overview   129

    Publications by John Wijngaards   133

    Bibliography   135

Introduction

ON WHY I WROTE THIS BOOKLET

OUR MIND NEEDS TO be fed. We need 'food for thought'. And our mind must *digest* this food, not just look at it: even salt looks like sugar. This booklet offers daily mind-feeding reflections for a month. I wrote it especially for all the many men and women who minister in the Catholic Church and other Churches. The ponderings will also benefit others who promote the welfare of the faithful: lecturers, teachers, journalists, doctors, nurses, members of pastoral councils and whoever else.

Because I value ministry in the Church, I am dismayed by the ugly accretions that have attached themselves to it in the course of the centuries. Like weeds, scallops and rubbish clinging to the bottom of a ship. I am thinking of unchristian cultural views, customs and practices from the Roman Empire, the barbarian tribes in Europe and the feudalistic Middle Ages that nailed themselves to the ministries. These cancerous growths were even enshrined in church laws . . .

That is why I wrote this booklet. The authority in the Church which Jesus gave can, in many amazing forms, bring life to every believer. I want us all to reflect on how that authority is exercised in the Church today—to unmask the accretions and rediscover what Jesus had in mind.

ON THE METHODOLOGY I
USE IN THIS BOOKLET

All of us have had the opportunity, and often duty, of teaching others. But have you thought about the widely divergent systems we can employ? I remember Myra, a primary school teacher I used to know, once saying to me: "Before I can teach my youngsters the ABC, I usually have to teach them how to properly use the toilet. . ."

Schools introduce children to **systematic/academic learning**. Academic teaching commonly presents a sequence of lessons progressing from what is simple to what is more complex. It attempts to drill rules into the mind. It helps students look at a problem logically. It offers mental tools such as diagrams, graphs, schemes, mathematical tables, chemical formulas, charts and maps. It aims at instilling in the student's mind a coherent picture of a topic, so that he or she can then assess and use practical applications in a coherent way. A person can then, for instance, construct his or her relationships in a 'family tree', a pyramid of lines with faces on the junctures where the lines meet.

However, the more normal human way of making sense of things comes through **reality learning**, that is: learning from everyday experience. It is the method I use in this booklet.

The vital role of reality learning was first recognised by early champions such as Maria Montessori and Jean Piaget. It has now been explored by many others. Reality learning is not organised. It arises from a patchwork of piecemeal encounters.

Think about it. Children learn to speak through reality learning. As they look at people's faces, they hear sounds. They notice the context—a smile, food, a cat or whatever—and then, suddenly it makes sense. The child links the particular person or object to a specific sound . . . Jean Piaget studied the many stages of mental development and language learning children go through.

And reality learning continues in later life. After and next to their academic study, medical doctors learn from dealing with their patients, salesmen from their customers, teachers from their students, priests from their parishioners, etc. Just having an experience is not enough. The important thing is that the experience is somehow reflected on and its lesson absorbed.

And we should note that this is also how Jesus taught. He did not present a systematic 'catechism' of his message. He used parables to intrigue a new audience. He proclaimed a new future in synagogues. He commented on events, like when picking corn on a Sabbath or after curing the man born blind. He argued with scribes and pharisees. He presented startling new ideas when invited to people's homes. His teaching was always somehow linked to the actual experience.

This explains why the series is designed in its specific form.

HOW TO MAKE MOST OF EACH CHAPTER

Each chapter consists of four separate, but interlinking parts.

At the start of each chapter you will find **a comic drawing, a cartoon, a caricature**. It depicts a particular situation in a funny way. It exaggerates. It distorts. It makes you laugh, or at least smile. Yes, this is comedy. But do not underestimate it. The best kind of comedy makes fun of a serious issue. Politicians often fear comedy. Mrs Thatcher, the Iron Lady, the UK's prime minister who could shout down opponents in parliament, dreaded jokes made about her in comedy shows and through caricatures printed in Britain's national newspapers. So even after having digested the other parts have another look again at the caricature and the concern it exposes.

This is followed by a **real-life story.** Through a short narrative I provide an example of how authority is exercised in the Church today. I am speaking about real events, things I have witnessed with my own eyes. Some of these events are praiseworthy. Others show up worrying defects. I would like you to examine your own experience at this stage. Do you think my story rings true? Have you seen or heard the same situation I am describing? I remember that on one occasion I was telling a group of women about an English parish priest who boasted publicly: "I will never tolerate a womb on my pulpit!" One of the women in the group, who was from Australia then told us about a similar insult she had heard from Cardinal Pell, Archbishop of Sydney. He stated: "Ordain a woman? You might as well try to ordain a potato!"

Then we consider how **Jesus** would have judged the situation. Now it is obvious that the conditions we live in differ from those Jesus faced. But the Gospels offer many parallels in spite of such differences. They help us see how Jesus dealt with challenges that often closely match the ones encountered by ministers in the Church today. Usually they offer clear evidence on what Jesus would want our response to be. Jesus cares profoundly about how the authority he transferred to us is handled by us. Jesus gave power to preach love, not power to instil fear; power to heal, not to inflict wounds; power to liberate, not power to enslave; power to serve, not power to dominate. Moreover, foreseeing the changes in times to come, Jesus promised that his Spirit would continue to guide us and to open our eyes to the implications of his earlier teaching. And his Spirit speaks through our prophets and teachers today, as well through the 'sense of faith' in the heart of every believer.

I conclude every chapter with a section entitled '**Questions**'. This part is meant for each person to identify the issues and problems at stake from his or her own perspective. It analyses the validity of Church practice. It also leads to self-examination. I have deliberately kept this section short. I just spell out some of the most obvious issues that need to be explored. My intention is that you, the reader, will now take over. Take time to reflect. Ponder on the message in the story, the Gospel texts, the caricature. Ask yourself: "Do I agree? Do I recognise the web of cultural beliefs and practices that foul and smudge the authority Jesus gave? If so, how does it affect me? How can the anomaly be remedied? What can I do to bring about the required reform, if reform is called for?"

CREDENTIALS OF THE STORYTELLER

Who am I to present tales of my experiences and offer my thoughts? My Master's Degree at the Biblical Institute and Doctorate at the Gregorian University both in Rome equipped me for my task as a theologian. It set me off on further research resulting in my publishing a menu of 34 books mainly on biblical spirituality. And my ministry made me serve on a truly international level. I taught future priests in St John's Major Seminary in Hyderabad, India, for 14 years. I taught African students at the Missionary Institute London for 20 years. As Vicar General of the Mill Hill Missionaries for 6 years I regularly visited 9 countries in Europe and North America. Journeys as a part-time lecturer and as producer of videos for adult catechesis made me familiar with countries in Asia (Pakistan, Indonesia, the Philippines), Africa (Uganda, Kenya, Ghana, Nigeria) and South America (Brazil, Colombia, Chile).

I have great admiration for the marvellous work achieved by bishops, priests, deacons and all other men and women in Church ministries. I have seen how their great personal sacrifices help hundreds of millions of people throughout the world: through parish services, education, health care, and development projects. I am proud of the many individuals whom I may have helped to perform their service—and some of whom have excelled.

Eight of the seminarians I instructed in Hyderabad, India, became bishops. Two religious Sisters whom I taught and for whom I mediated studies at a university in Rome became General Superiors of their Congregations. My Mill Hill classmate Piet Vos gave his life for the parishioners of Lingomo in Zaire. This happened on the 27th of November 1964 when he tried to protect his people against communist rebels who overran the region. Father Christian Chessel, a 'Missionary of Africa' student whom I taught at the Missionary Institute London, was executed by Muslims on the 27th of December 1994 in Tizi-Ouzou, Algeria. To obtain his master's degree in theology he had written a dissertation for me on 'Consolation at death as portrayed in the Pauline Letters'. He will be one of twenty missionary martyrs to be beatified by Pope Francis in December 2023. I have truly tried to support ministers throughout my life.

OVER TO YOU!

I designed this booklet as a help for reflection and to promote reforms. It contains 28 chapters spread out over four weeks, so it lasts for a month. You will find that the chapters gradually present more stringent problems as the series moves on.

I recommend that you focus on one chapter each day. Do not give in to the temptation to look ahead and try to absorb too much in one go. You will benefit more if you reserve all attention to that day's chapter. But if you seek integration at the same time, there is of course no harm in relating the day's issue to what you have reflected on in previous chapters.

Well, give it a go! The proof of the pudding is in the eating. A Chinese proverb states: 'If it looks daft but it works, it isn't daft for you'. Or as the Spanish say, 'Wear the cloth. Only then you can judge it'.

1

Power? Yes, but . . .

Jesus taught as one who has authority and not as their scribes. (Matt 7:29)

Who hears you, hears me. Who rejects you, rejects me. And he who rejects me, rejects the one who sent me. (Luke 10:16)

© Wijngaards Institute

"Don't shiver! I'm your parish priest. I'll tell you whether it's hot or cold!"

THERE WAS A TIME in the Netherlands when priests from local parishes were expected to give catechism classes in Catholic high schools.

I recall the agony suffered by a colleague of mine who had just been ordained for the diocese of s'-Hertogenbosch. He had been appointed to the parish of Mill, a large predominantly Catholic village in the province of Brabant. I too served in that parish for a few weeks to stand in for a priest who was on holidays. That is why I could witness his struggles first hand. It was the end of summer 1962.

We cycled together to the high school to give religious instruction. We taught in adjoining classrooms. If I remember well, level two students were entrusted to him, level three to me.

As I addressed the students, some at the back kept talking to each other. I banged my fist on the teacher's lectern and shouted at them. They immediately fell in line. But soon I heard loud noises from my colleague's classroom. There was laughing, and I heard crashes. So I temporarily left my own classroom and looked through a side window at what was going on next door. Chaos! Students standing on their seats shouting at each other and throwing books. My colleague standing helpless at his lectern in front of the class, raising his arms but to no effect. Believe me, it is true!

When I saw the principal running up from his office to restore order I quickly went back to my own classroom. At the end of my teaching session I met the principal who told me the other priest had already returned to the presbytery.

"What went wrong?," I asked.

"Well," he said, shrugging his shoulders. "Your friend does not have what it takes. He does not take *charge*. He is not a natural leader. The boys sense that and take advantage . . ."

LEADERSHIP, NATURAL AND COMMISSIONED

It is useful to reflect on the relationship between our personality and our authority. Sociology tells us that any community or group tends to be guided by so-called 'natural leaders'. These are persons who possess the qualities required to inspire and lead others. Among such qualities we may reckon: the ability to maintain good human relations; a special talent in the skills demanded by the group; maturity of character; and a sense of responsibility. Whereas others may try to command respect in vain, natural leaders will spontaneously be recognised and accepted by the group.

Without any doubt Jesus himself was a natural leader. But he acted because he had been commissioned. He proclaimed a message on the strength of authority given him. Contemporaries noted he was not talking like their scribes. "You have heard that it was said . . ., but I say to you. . ." (Matt 5:21.27.31.33.38.43). "I say to you!" Jesus knew himself assigned to his task by God and empowered with authority.

Jesus' authority manifested itself also in his miraculous cures and in his power to forgive sins. Confronted with the priests in the temple, Jesus insisted on possessing authority to drive out the merchants. Jesus sent his apostles into the whole world in the awareness: "To me has been given all authority in heaven and on earth" (Matt 28:18). But what about the apostles? Were they chosen by Jesus because they had social qualities conducive to make them accepted as natural leaders?

We know that Jesus selected the apostles very carefully. Before calling the twelve, Jesus prayed the whole night. He chose only those "whom he himself selected." Studying the gospels, we find plenty of indications to show that Jesus did not only select them on a spiritual basis, but also with an eye on their natural talents. Some degree of natural leadership was undoubtedly presupposed in Jesus' selection of the apostles. But the authority Jesus gave may not be judged as an extension of such natural dispositions. Jesus gave something startlingly new and entirely different.

THE KIND OF AUTHORITY JESUS GAVE

There can be no doubt that, in the history of the church, the apostles' successors often got things wrong in their exercise of authority. Church governance needs to be reformed. However, in doing so the true authority of church leaders should not be lost or minimised. This requires careful scrutiny.

QUESTIONS

1. What is your own experience of people performing ministries in the Church? Do they possess the natural talents required for leadership? Do they enjoy the skill to relate to each person according to his or her need?

2. How do you think Jesus would have tried to support them?

3. And what can you do about it?

2

Power to spread God's Kingdom

"Go and proclaim that the kingdom of heaven has come near. Heal the sick, raise the dead, cleanse those who have leprosy, drive out demons." (Matt 10:7)

"The kingdom of God is not coming with external signs. People will not say:'See, it is here!' or 'See, it is there!' For the kingdom of God is within you." (Luke 17:20–21)

© Wijngaards Institute

"Says he's from planet Earth. Looking for the Kingdom of Heaven."

IN 1961, WHEN I was studying for my doctorate in Rome, I attended the ordination of a priest from Bafut in Northwest Cameroon.

5

His name was Pius Suh Awa. I met him a couple of times in the *Propaganda Fide College* where he was staying at the time.

Twelve years later Pius was to become bishop of Buea diocese in Cameroon, but I want to narrate one of his achievements. As a young local priest Pius was appointed curate of Fiango Parish, Kumba, and later supervisor of Catholic schools in the Forest Area of West Cameroon. Pius was one of the sons of the 'Fon', the local king of the Bafut tribe. For more than a century there had been frequent fights between the Bafuts and other local tribes, such as the Mankons, the Metas and the Mungakas. Pius's new position gave him a unique opportunity.

On a number of occasions, when in certain villages fights between the neighbouring tribes were flaring up, Pius intervened. He called both parties together, led them in negotiations and then proclaimed peace. His authority was recognised, both as a son of the Bafuts' Fon and as an ordained priest. The parties gave in. Peace prevailed. Pius had acted as an official herald of peace.

I find it significant that he chose for his episcopal motto, displayed on his coat of arms, the latin words "Ut Cognoscant Te." It means: "That they may know Thee." He rightly saw his task as making his people truly understand God.

WHAT DOES 'HERALDS OF GOD'S KINGDOM' MEAN?

Let us begin with the expression 'the kingdom of heaven'. For Jesus it stands for the new reality his Father was going to bring about. In 'kingdom of heaven', *heaven* stands for God. This can be seen from the many instances in which the Gospels mention ‹kingdom of *God*' as an obvious equivalent. To avoid mentioning God by name, the Jews often used 'heaven' when they meant 'God'. They would say: 'I have sinned against heaven' and 'we don't know whether this comes from heaven or from human beings'. Think also of our own expression: 'Heaven forbid!' Kingdom of heaven therefore means: God's kingdom.

The word *kingdom* needs clarification too. When we speak about a kingdom, we usually think of a country that is ruled by a king. We can then say that someone travelled the length and breadth of the kingdom, or that there was a war between two kingdoms, and so on. This was not the first and most important meaning of *malkûth*, 'kingdom', for the Jews. *Malkûth* meant someone's 'being king', what we may render by kingship in English. God's kingship means that God rules as king.

There are very few kings or queens left in the world and where they still exist they are, to a great extent, no more than figure-heads of national unity. For most of us it is easy to forget how central the position of a king was in ancient society.

In tribal societies like Israel, the community resembled a large family and the king was an overall father; possessing, as father, absolute power and ultimate responsibility. Under a good king the whole family of society flourished; under a bad king everyone suffered hardship. The king was at once lawgiver, supreme judge and army chief. In Israel, in spite of influences from neighbouring nations, the tribal image of a king who is close at hand and paternalistic remained predominant.

It is clear from the Gospel that for Jesus God's kingship brought a new reality to human society. It established neighbourly friendship, peace, tolerance, forgiveness, self sacrifice, care for those in need, in short: a realm of love.

HERALDS OF GOD'S KINGDOM

Remember that in Jesus' time TV, radio, the press did not exist. Whenever a political reality changed, the population would be informed about this by officially appointed 'heralds' who would proclaim what was happening. Roman 'heralds' proclaimed that Emperor Cesar Augustus had decreed a registration of the whole population of Syria, to which Palestine belonged at the time. It required people to travel to their town of origin. This was the decree that made Joseph and Mary travel from Nazareth in Galilee to Bethlehem in Judea, since Joseph was a descendant of David (Luke 2:1–5).

It is obvious that not just anyone could act as a herald. A person had to be officially appointed, authorised, to act as a herald. Heralds were authorised to carry state messages or to make proclamations. We should realise that a political proclamation brought about a tangible result. Something changed. Once Pontius Pilate had been proclaimed Roman procurator in a town or village, his rule over that area had been established.

Jesus chose twelve disciples and appointed them 'heralds' of God's new Kingdom. The Greek word 'apostle' actually means 'a herald'. The main task of the apostles, and of their successors: popes, bishops and priests, is to bring about God's kingship among people. And in the beginning the new reality was made visible through miracles of healing. "Go and proclaim that the kingdom of heaven has come near. Heal the sick, raise the dead, cleanse those who have leprosy, drive out demons" (Matt 10:8).

These initial signs pointed to the inner healing that was Jesus' real purpose. This spiritual healing would transform people. As the beatitudes express it, it would make people humble in spirit, meek, thirsting for what is right, merciful, pure in heart, peacemakers, ready to suffer for the cause of righteousness.

QUESTIONS

1. What are your experiences of ministries in the Church? Were they positive, negative? Did you find that ministry is first and foremost focussed on bringing about that inner, spiritual transformation in people? Or is it too much preoccupied with the externals of governance, with burocracy, with imposing rules, with administration?

2. How do you personally think Jesus would have assessed the situation?

3. Is there anything you can do about it?

3

Power of the keys

(Jesus said to Cephas:): "And I tell you, you are Peter (rock), and on this rock I will build my assembly (church). The powers of death shall not prevail against it. I will give you the keys of the kingdom of heaven." (Matt 16: 18–19)

(Jesus said to the Scribes:): "Woe to you experts in the law, because you have taken away the key to knowledge. You yourselves have not entered, and you have hindered those who were entering." (Luke 11:51)

© Wijngaards Institute

"Lost your key, Father? Just ring the bell. As your housekeeper it's I who have the power of the keys!"

In the 1980's as Vicar General of the Mill Hill Missionaries I visited Kampala in Uganda, an archdiocese in which a number of our members served. A three-day gathering had been organised in a retreat centre near the capital.

On the closing day, at supper, something interesting happened. One of our older fathers, whom I shall call 'Jo' and who served as parish priest in a remote village, stood up from his seat at table and addressed the community. He had been known for his forgetfulness. On a previous occasion he had returned to his mission station without leaving the key to his bedroom in the retreat centre . . .

"Friends," he told us. "It's time for me to depart. As you know it takes four hours for me to reach my place. Well, to correct my reputation," and with this he swayed around a key for all to see. "With all of you as witnesses I am solemnly returning the key to my room!"

He stepped forward to where the local superior was sitting ready to hand him the key.

"Thanks, Jo! Unbelievable!," the superior said. "Just dump it on the tray over there!"

The old priest waved at everyone, took up his travel bag, left the dining room and soon afterwards we heard his jeep take off for the journey.

It was not the end of the story. After the meal the superior strolled over to the tray onto which others too had dumped their keys. Picking up one of them, he exclaimed: "Goodness! Jo has done it again! He has left the key of his own house!"

It meant that poor Jo, arriving in the middle of the night at his parish house in that far-away place would find he was carrying the wrong key . . .

WHAT POWER DID JESUS GIVE?

There is no doubt that Jesus gave authority to Peter, the head of the apostolic team, and by implication to his successors, popes and bishops included. In imperial Roman times and the feudal Middle

Ages this was soon interpreted as Peter having somehow been elevated to the rank of 'emperor' of the international Christian community. But is this what Jesus intended?

The words "I will build my *ecclesia*" have misled many to take for granted that 'ecclesia' would refer to a building, a structure, with all the connotations which the word 'church' has acquired in English. Jesus is indeed comparing the 'ecclesia' here to a house with the main purpose of stressing the foundation which he was giving it. Elsewhere he had employed the same metaphor when he taught that it would be wise to build one's life not on sand, but on the firm rock of his teaching (Matt 7:24–26). Just as one's life is not a house or a structure, so also the 'ecclesia', the 'church' should be taken to mean a house or a structure only in a metaphorical sense. In New Testament time 'ecclesia' simply stood for 'assembly', 'community'.

The 'power of the keys' does not refer to overall top-down command. In Jesus' world it was not the emperors, the kings, the governors who were key holders. Key holders were functionaries who could grant access to sacred premises, state properties or large estates. Peter's 'power of the keys' refers to opening the doors of knowledge, to teaching.

Jesus reproves the scribes for having deprived the people of the 'key to knowledge' (Luke 11:52). Remember that Jesus sent the apostles to preach the good news that his Father's kingdom, the 'kingdom of heaven', had arrived. It did not refer to a place after death but to a new realm on earth where peace, forgiveness, reconciliation, love could flourish. By his authoritative teaching on this new spiritual reality Peter and his companions and their successors would give people access to a sublime sphere of love.

QUESTION

1. What is your personal experiences with regard to the meaning of authority in the Church? Positive, negative? Did you

find it is perceived as control from above or a spiritual power to give people access to a sublime sphere of love?

2. How do you personally think Jesus would have assessed the situation?

3. Is there anything you can do about it?

4

Power to bind or to loosen

"Truly I tell you, whatever you bind on earth will be bound in heaven, and whatever you loosen on earth will be loosened in heaven." (Matt 18:18)

"Does [a master] thank his slave because he did what he was told? So you also, when you have done everything commanded of you, should say, 'We are unworthy slaves; we have only done our duty." (Luke 17:9–10)

"Stop moaning! Be proud of your role in our splendid Roman navy!"

IN THE 1980's I used to lecture on Sacred Scripture at the Missionary Institute London. When discussing the dreadful misunderstanding of texts on slavery I always experienced an emotional response from my students. Many hailed from Africa where memories of the colonial slave trade have left painful wounds.

One time, during our lunch break, one of my students came to talk to me. He was a Filipino. Taking his seat next to me at table, he told me the following story.

"I come from the island of Iloilo, but I studied philosophy in a major seminary in Manila. Every year we were sent for a month's pastoral formation to a local parish. There I saw a terrible thing."

"What was it?" I asked him.

"Well, the parish priest wanted to extend the cemetery. But when they started digging in a field just outside the cemetery wall, they found heaps of ancient human skeletons just dumped like rubbish into holes in the ground."

"Horrible," I said. "But strange. The Spanish usually treated their dead well."

"Yes. But these were not Spaniards. An archaeologist identified them as African, male and female. Bruises on their bones showed they had been slaves . . . I later found out that the Spanish colonists in the 16th and 17th centuries were not allowed to keep local people as slaves, since all inhabitants of the Philippines had been declared Spanish citizens. So they started importing slaves from Africa. Around 1650 AD every Spanish household in Manila had one or two African slaves. And this was done by practising Catholics . . ."

BINDING OR LOOSENING

Jesus' words "whatever you bind on earth will be bound in heaven" are truly momentous. Binding or loosening apply to obligations people have. Binding refers to forbidding something, loosening to permitting it. The Jewish tradition preserved in the Mishnah defines to bind as 'to forbid by an indisputable authority' and to loosen as 'to permit by an indisputable authority'.

The assertion that the obligation is sanctioned 'in heaven' ties it to the highest possible spiritual authority. For 'in heaven' is simply a Jewish manner of speaking in order to avoid mentioning

God by name. "Whatever you bind on earth will be bound in heaven" means "whatever you bind on earth will be bound in God's eyes too."

Jesus appointed the apostles and their successors to guide people in their quest of God's new realm of love. Part of that guidance was to consist in telling them, authoritatively, what was allowed and what was not.

A POWER FRAUGHT WITH DANGER

Authoritative guidance can be a great help to people who sincerely want to do God's will in difficult circumstances. It can relieve them of a sense of guilt in complex moral situations. It lifted an enormous burden from Christian converts in 50 AD when the first General Council, the Council of Jerusalem, decided that the Old Testament law, the Torah, did not bind them. But it is obvious that Jesus did not want his apostles and their successors to use the binding and loosening power light-heartedly. He calls the scribes and Pharisees of his time 'blind guides' for all the erroneous obligations they imposed on people (Matt 23:16–26).

And, sadly, the history of the Church shows that popes and bishops have often made crucial mistakes when exercising their power to bind or loosen. One of them is the case of slavery.

IS SLAVERY ALLOWED?

Slavery was common in the Roman, Hellenistic and Jewish world of Jesus' time. Jesus taught through parables. On one occasion, when teaching the need of humility in the presence of God, he holds out this comparison: "Does [a master] thank his slave because he did what he was told? So you also, when you have done everything commanded of you, should say, 'We are unworthy slaves; we have only done our duty.'" (Luke 17:9–10)

Did Jesus hereby teach that slavery of a human being by someone else is allowed? Of course, not. As little as he was permitting cheating when presenting the parable of the unjust steward (Luke 16:1–13). The point of the parable is that we should use our intelligence. Jesus warned that on the last day 'the Son of Man will come as a thief in the night' (Matt 24:43). Did he thereby condone stealing or burglary? No, the point of the comparison is that his coming will be totally unexpected.

Did Jesus condemn slavery? you may ask. No, he did not, at least not explicitly. Jesus sided with the underdogs, the poor, the deprived. He healed slaves as well as lepers and other outcasts. But he did not explicitly take up the causes of social reform, such as racism, the emancipation of women, the abolition of absolute totalitarian rule and-so-on. Such human rights were implicitly contained in what Jesus did and taught. He established that one and the same rite of baptism would apply to all disciples. He invited all to the same eucharistic meal. He did not lay down limits as to who could minister in his community.

Unfortunately, church leaders have often made mistakes when exercising their power to bind or loosen. Slavery is a tragic example. Basing themselves on Jesus' text on a slave's humility quoted above and some equally misunderstood passages in St Paul's Letters, Popes defended the legitimacy of slavery in one century after the other. In 1866 Pope Pius IX still taught: "*Slavery is not at all contrary to the natural and divine law . . . It is not contrary to the natural and divine law for a slave to be sold, bought, exchanged or given.*"[1]

QUESTIONS

1. Based on your experience, do you believe that Church leaders sufficiently acknowledge that errors were proclaimed in the past, including many by Popes? How do you think such errors should be prevented in the future?

2. What would Jesus have done about this? And what about yourself, is there anything you can do about it?

1. Pius IX, "Instruction on Slavery," in Maxwell, "Development of Catholic Doctrine," 306–7.

5

Power to forgive sins

Jesus said, "As the Father has sent me, I am sending you . . . If you forgive anyone's sins, their sins are forgiven!" (John 20:21)

© Wijngaards Institute

"I hope you're not in a hurry, Father. My last confession was forty years ago!"

LET ME START WITH a true story. I remember it like the day of yesterday though it happened a long time ago—in the 1960's.

I was visiting a friend of mine, the Rev Robert Marsh, in his home on Abids Road, Secunderabad, India. Robert was the local Vicar for the Church of South India. As we were having a cup of tea in his lounge, an acquaintance of his passed by who ministered as an evangelical preacher.

When the preacher discovered that I was a Catholic priest, he launched an attack. "You priests claim you can forgive sins, don't you?"

"Yes," I replied.

"Well, that is the height of Catholic arrogance! Just think of it. God is the almighty ruler of the universe and sins are offences *against him*. Admit: offences against the highest power that exists. And you claim you can forgive them!"

"Jesus gave us authority to do so," I said.

"Did he? Prove it to me!"

I asked Robert Marsh for a copy of his Bible. Then I read out this passage from Jesus' appearance to the apostles after his resurrection.

> 'Jesus said, "Peace be with you! As the Father has sent me, I am sending you." And with that he breathed on them and said, "Receive the Holy Spirit. If you forgive anyone's sins, their sins are forgiven; if you do not forgive them, they are not forgiven."' (John 20:21–23)

It stunned him. "I've never come across that passage," he stammered. He grabbed the Bible from my hands to see whether the text was truly there.

FORGIVING SINS

The Gospel of Luke narrates an incident in Jesus' life that is truly revealing (Luke 5:17–26). Jesus was teaching inside a house. Crowds surrounded him both inside the building and in the adjoining courtyard. Some men approached carrying a paralysed man on a litter. They did not know how to get their friend to Jesus. In the end they found a solution. They walked up a staircase at the back of the house and reached the flat roof. They then removed some flagstones from the roof, creating a hole through which they lowered the man in front of Jesus' feet.

Commotion! But Jesus appreciated their faith. He must have talked to the paralytic. Then he told him: "Your sins are forgiven."

Some scribes and Pharisees who were present in the room were scandalised. "How can he presume to forgive sins? Only God can forgive sins!"

Jesus turned to them and said: "To show you that I have power to forgive sins on earth in the name of God, see what I am doing now!" He told the paralysed man: "Stand up. Take up the litter and go home!" That is what the man did.

Being able to forgive sins in God's name is indeed extraordinary. Yes, Jesus gave his ministers incredible authority. This authority even devolves to all of his followers in special circumstances, as I will show in a later reflection. But it is worth reflecting on what kind of authority it is.

QUESTIONS

1. Do you think ministers are sufficiently aware of the fact that church authority is *spiritual* authority? That means a different sort of authority, authority that derives from 'God', the deepest dimension underlying the universe, the mysterious power that pervades reality as we know it? What is your own experiences about this? Positive, negative, or mixed?

2. What would Jesus have done in the circumstances? And is there anything you can do about it?

6

Power to save lives

"I am sending you, just as the Father has sent me." (John 20:21)

"Whoever hears you hears me. Whoever rejects you rejects me, and who rejects me rejects the One who sent me." (Luke 10:16)

© Wijngaards Institute

"I know you can read God's mind, Father. Should I switch to investing in oil?"

DURING MY SPELL AS Vicar General of the Mill Hill Missionaries I would visit our houses in the USA every year. I would then also meet some of our returned missionaries, who at the time of retirement had opted to continue some form of pastoral work. One of them was a Dutch missionary whom I shall call 'Jim'. He had served for almost forty years in Central Africa. On retirement he was happy to accept the assignment to a parish in Manhattan where his main task consisted in being chaplain to a local hospital.

The hospital was 14 storeys high. Every day Jim, using a walking stick, would go round as many wards as he could, moving up from one storey to the next.

"My work is amazing," Jim told me. "I take holy communion to many people, but it doesn't stop there. As I move from bed to bed I come across many Catholics in need of special attention. Some have problems at home. Some haven't been to church for many years because of one reason or another. Some are tormented by doubts. Some are troubled in their conscience because of things they have done."

"So, you can really help them," I said.

"Yes, yes, I can. At times it leads to full-fledged confession, more often it only needs a frank discussion which helps them resolve inner conflict."

"Great!," I told him.

"Indeed. Often it is hard for me—walking all that distance inside the hospital at my age. Moreover, walking back home from the hospital to the parish which is often late in the evening I got mugged twice. Thrown down onto the pavement. My briefcase snatched from my hand, wallet from my pocket. It was a shock I tell you. But—it doesn't stop me."

He then leant over to me. "I've done good work in Africa, you know. But this is even better. I can talk to people from person to person, as Jesus would have done. In his name I can resolve issues. Never in my life have I felt so much *a priest* as I'm doing here these days."

AMBASSADORS OF GOD

We have seen in an earlier meditation that the term 'apostle', that is 'someone who is sent', could apply to public heralds, persons empowered to proclaim a new political reality to the public. 'Apostle' stands also for 'ambassador'. Someone commissioned to meet a specific person and delegated to act and speak on behalf of a ruler.

Fast modes of communication that we use in our own time: phone calls, telegrams, twitter, email and-so-on did not exist in Jesus' time. When the Roman Emperor sent an ambassador to a king in the North of Europe or in the Middle East, that person had to be empowered to negotiate the terms of peace or surrender, or details of a trade deal by himself. The ambassador was commissioned to resolve often complex issues in the name of the authority that sent him.

This means that when the ambassador met the individual he was sent to, he could authoritatively convey the mind and the voice of his master.

Dealing with individuals he met, Jesus acted like the ambassador of his Father. We have numerous examples of persons who benefitted from such a personal encounter:

- people whom he invited to join him, such as fishermen Simon and Andrew, farmer Nathanael and tollbooth manager Matthew;

- outcasts infected with leprosy;

- the paralysed man dropped down in front of him through a hole in the roof;

- the man with a shrivelled hand whom he met in a synagogue;

- Nicodemus who came to talk to Jesus at night;

- Zaccheus, the tax collector in Jericho;

- the widow of Naim who was on the way to bury her son;

- the paralysed man lying near the pool of Bethesda;

- the Roman officer in Capernaum whose slave was ill;

- the anxious mother in Syro-Phoenicia whose daughter was possessed by an impure spirit;

- the woman from Samaria who came to draw water at the well where Jesus was resting;

- and others.

What does this mean for the successors of the apostles in our own day?

QUESTIONS

1. Do you agree that a general ministry to the multitude—through sermons at Sunday mass, brief sessions in the confessional or pastoral guidance in print—will not do? What are your thoughts about that?

2. Do you know priests and others in the ministry who create opportunities to meet people in person? Do they give time to listen to people's individual stories and solve their specific issues?

3. How do you think Jesus would judge the pastoral practice you are familiar with?

4. Is there anything you can do to support or improve the practice?

7

Power to drive out mental demons

"I have given you authority to tread on snakes and scorpions, and over all the power of the enemy. Nothing will harm you. Nevertheless, do not rejoice that demons submit to you, but rejoice that your names are written in heaven." (Luke 10:19–20)

© Wijngaards Institute

"Hey brother. If we infest this guy, we'll never be short of bucks!"

THIS IS A SAD story, based on true facts.

During one of my trips to the United States I visited a wealthy Chicago businessman and his wife. Their son Phil had served as a Catholic priest for a number of years. Then things went awry.

"He came to us," his father told me, holding his arm round his wife's shoulder. She was crying. "We knew there was something terribly wrong. He would flare up one moment with anger, then he would sit in a corner of the room sobbing and wiping his eyes. At night he couldn't sleep. He kept walking around in our garden."

"Did you try to find out what was troubling him?," I asked.

"Yes, we did. No luck. He wouldn't talk to us. I made an appointment with a psychiatrist. It didn't work. In the end our parish priest arranged a session with the diocesan exorcist. It was a disaster. Phil was furious. He ran out, shouting at all of us . . ."

"And then, worst of all, he came home and went up to his room. Later we found him dead in the bathroom. He had hanged himself . . ."

I tried to console the couple as well as I could. I had already heard from other sources what had been behind it all. Phil had fallen in love with a young woman. Then when he discovered she was pregnant, he simply did not know what to do. He did not find the right person to help him through the predicament he was in. Yes, it truly happened.

DEMONS IN THE GOSPEL ACCOUNTS

At the time Jesus lived in Palestine, people ascribed defects in animals or humans to being afflicted by demons, unclean spirits. It was a belief that had been inherited by the Jews from civilizations in Mesopotamia. Remember that the action of infections by bacteria or viruses had not yet been discovered.

Unclean spirits were not considered devils. People were aware of the fact that some inner forces are at work within a physical body: the 'psyche' that keeps the body alive and, in humans, the 'pneuma', the deeper human soul. Demons were reckoned to be strange unhealthy 'psyches' that travelled around looking for a body to infest. Mental illness too in a man or a woman was blamed on an invasion by such demons.

Jesus accepted this belief of his time. 'Driving out someone's unclean spirits' was equivalent to curing that person. For Jesus this was not just an external ritual. It implied also relating to that person, treating him or her as an individual who needs support.

Most healing accounts in the Gospels have been reduced to a minimum. They were part of the oral catechetical tradition before they were written down in text. So we often get the impression that Jesus just cured a person and then left them to their own devices. This, we can be sure, is not correct. It is confirmed in the more elaborate story of a man afflicted by unclean spirits who lived in the region of the Gerasenes on the other side of the Sea of Galilee (Mark 5:1–20).

We are told that the poor man would stay in cemeteries or roam in deserted areas, day and night not wearing any clothes. He would cry out in anguish and cut himself with stones. He obviously was mentally disturbed.

When Jesus had driven a 'legion' of demons out of him, the man put on a dress and sat down with Jesus. Astonished neighbours found that the man had recovered 'his right mind'. When Jesus and other disciples entered a boat to cross the Sea of Galilee, he begged Jesus for permission to come along. He must have said: "I want to be one of your disciples. I can help you in your work!"

Aware of the man's mental instability, Jesus did not consider this a wise move. The man needed a more prolonged and full recovery with his relatives at home. So Jesus gently gave him this advice: "No. Rather go back home to your family. There too you will have opportunities to preach the Good News. Tell them how God has shown mercy to you and healed you by his power!"

COUNSELING

Many people also in our own days struggle with mental health problems. Priests can be of enormous help to them but it requires the fundamental skills of understanding people and how to counsel them. These are some of the 'unclean spirits' they will come across:

- The demon of *guilt*. "I have messed things up. Should have done better. Nothing can undo the harm I've caused."

- The demon of *anxiety*. "I can't cope. I fear the worst. I panic about everything. I don't know what to do."

- The demon of *downgrading oneself*. "I'm worth nothing. Small wonder people ignore me. I'm really a nobody. I've got nothing I can be proud of."

- The demon of *depression*. "I feel hopeless, worthless., exhausted. I can't sleep. I've lost my appetite. I'm at a loss what to do."

QUESTIONS

1. What is your personal experience? Did you find that priests realise that they, without underestimating the expertise of professional psychiatrists, can and should make their own contribution to mental healing?

2. Have you seen priests wipe away guilt, reassure waverers, put those who stray back on the right path? Priests who speak in the name of God who is love?

3. If Jesus witnessed what you did, would he have applauded or deplored the events?

4. Is there anything you can do to reinforce or improve matters?

8

Power to liberate

"In saying this Jesus declared all foods clean." (Mark 7:19)

"Jesus straightened up and said to her, "Where are they, woman? Is there no one left to condemn you? "No one, sir," she answered. "Well, then," Jesus said, "I do not condemn you either. You may leave, but do not sin again." (John 8:10–11)

© Wijngaards Institute

Brother George says it is a mortal sin to work in our vegetable garden on Sundays.

THERE WAS A TIME—AND not so long ago—that Catholic life was dominated by fear of incurring a 'mortal sin'. Mortal sin, we were taught, would be punished by being condemned to burn in hell

28

forever, unless you obtained forgiveness before you died. Let me share a horrifying experience of it in my own life when I was ten years old.

It was December 1945. With my mother and three brothers I had been detained for four and a half years in Japanese prisoner-of-war camps. Non-stop hunger with one small meal a day. Ever recurring diseases without proper medication. Constant fear of our guards' brutality.

On the 15th of August 1945 Japan had surrendered. We were at the time in Camp Ambarawa 6 in central Java, then part of the Dutch East Indies. Instead of improving, our situation worsened because Javanese rebel groups encircled the camp from all sides. A platoon of Gurkha soldiers from the British army was parachuted in. They protected our camp. But they could not prevent the camp being shelled from surrounding hills causing daily casualties. Food was scarce, depending on supplies being dropped from the skies by RAF planes. Our drink water was cut off from time to time causing agony in the tropical heat.

Our predicament lasted for three and a half months. Finally on the 5th of December a British military convoy fought their way from the coast to our camp. We were loaded on trucks and transported to the relative safety of liberated Halmahera camp in harbour town Semarang.

What about 'mortal sin', you may wonder? Well, listen. A few days after arrival in Halmahera we heard that next morning a Catholic priest would celebrate Mass in a nearby barrack. It was an event we had missed for a long time. We attended eagerly. When the moment of communion came round, I suddenly remembered that I had drunk some water in the middle of the night—I did not know the exact time. I recalled with anguish that during the instruction classes I had received before receiving my first holy communion, we had been told that after midnight eating or drinking before holy communion was forbidden under 'mortal sin'.

I did not know what to do. In the end, with fear and trembling, I joined my mother and received communion . . . And then a real agony of conscience gripped me. What if I had committed a *mortal* sin?! What should I do about it? I realised priests were scarce at that time. So while the crowd was leaving the barrack after mass, I slipped away from my mother and timidly approached the make-shift altar where the priest was packing up the sacred utensils. He was an elderly Dutch missionary.

"Father," I whispered, looking up at him. "I may have committed a mortal sin. Can I go to confession?"

"Fine," he said. He put on his stole and grabbed a stool to sit on. I knelt at his feet.

"What's the matter?," he said. I told him what had happened.

He looked at me. "Well, I am glad you take it seriously. But don't worry. I will give you absolution. So even if you *did* drink after midnight, all guilt is wiped away now!"

FREEDOM FROM LAW

Christ liberated us from sin. He gave his life to redeem us. He poured out his blood "for many for the forgiveness of sins." When Jesus was asked to explain what he meant by saying, "You will be made free", he answered: "I tell you the truth, everyone who sins is a slave of sin." The freedom which Jesus brought is first and foremost *a freedom from sin*.

To liberate us from slavery to sin, Jesus demolished the prison walls of external law. Time and again he disregarded and transgressed the laws that the Jews were being told to follow. In this respect Jesus was a real rebel and a liberator. He clashed frequently with the Jewish authorities by doing or by making others do, what had been forbidden on the Sabbath. The woman caught in adultery had to be stoned to death according to the law. Jesus simply sends her away without punishment. When arguing with the scribes about the traditions of the elders (concerning the washing of hands before taking a meal), Jesus not only rejected those traditions, but revoked the Old Testament law according to which some foods were clean and others unclean. "Nothing that goes into a person from the outside can make him unclean," Jesus proclaimed. His listeners understood that he declared all foods clean.

It would be wrong to imagine that Jesus did no more than rearrange the laws, abolishing some and promulgating others. He did not substitute a new code of laws for the old one. Wherever Jesus spoke about law, he replaced external performance by interior sanctity. The one obligation for Christians is love and all the implications that follow from it.

Jesus' disciples understood Jesus' revolutionary new morality.

1. "For freedom Christ has truly set us free. Now make sure that you stay free, and don't get tied up again in slavery to law . . . If you are led by the Spirit, you are not under any law." (Gal 5:1.18)

2. "In Christ Jesus the law of the Spirit of life has set you free from the law of sin and death." (Rom 8:2)

3. "As long as we love another God will live in us and God's love will be complete in us . . . In love there can be no fear. Fear is driven out by perfect love. Because to fear is to expect punishment, and anyone who is afraid is still imperfect in love." (1 John 4:12.18)

AUTHORITY THAT PROMOTES THE FREEDOM OF LOVE

Authority in the Catholic Church has relied on exercising control by imposing laws. Obligations imposed under mortal sin included attending Sunday mass, annual confession, not eating meat on Fridays, avoiding masturbation and divorce. Much of this has been relaxed after Vatican II, but the attitude still prevails. Recent Popes added other prohibitions such as the use of artificial means of contraception and homosexual acts.

QUESTIONS

1. Do Church leaders honour what was priority for Jesus? What is your personal experience in this matter? Does fear of transgressing a law and incurring sin predominate?

2. Do pastors focus on educating people to a spiritual transformation within their minds and hearts? Do they encourage people to live by unconditional love, to listen to the Spirit, to be faithful to their conscience?

3. How would Jesus judge the situation?

4. And if a new orientation in the ministry is needed, what can you do about it?

9

The authority of women

'When Jesus had given thanks, he broke the bread and said: "This is my body which is for you. Do this in memory of me." In the same way, after supper he took the cup, saying: "This cup is the new covenant in my blood. Do this, as often as you drink it, in memory of me."' (1 Cor 11:24–25)

"Wait till you see what Thomas Aquinas thought about women!"

I GOT TO KNOW Claire Daurelle, a French lay minister, who served from 1978 to 1999 in the diocese of Lyon, France. Trained as a catechist she was first put in charge of a chaplaincy. Later she was appointed to help a priest run a parish.

She described her work: "I preach. I conduct funerals. I can say with true honesty that I fulfil my function absolutely everywhere. I do exactly the same that the parish priest does. We share the work, the tasks, in an absolutely equal fashion, except for the sacramental rites. I prepare couples for marriage, and for the baptism of a child. I celebrate *with* the priest, though it requires his presence."

And then she mentions her thoughts about priestly ordination . . .

"During the summer which had preceded my arrival in the parish, the summer of 1987, a question appeared in me which was totally new and about which I had not strictly thought before: 'Why can't I be a priest?' I tried at first to avoid this question. I thought that it was a useless question because there was no solution in the Catholic Church. But as the question grew on me, I wrote about it to my bishop and I asked him for ordination. I received his answer by return post. I know it by heart. It ran as follows: 'I know that you know what the Catholic Church says with regard to this question. I do not want to add to it, but I ask you to live with it in faith'. I am trying to do so. I do as much as I can. And I can truly say that during the seven years from that moment until his death—Mgr. Decourtray died last year—this bishop has truly given me pastoral support with regard to that question. He has never taken me for granted. Every time when I telephoned him in order to arrange a meeting, he agreed to it immediately. For him it was very important to give me pastoral support in my priestly vocation. He never tried to extinguish it in me. He never told me: 'Think about something else. Forget about it.'"[1]

1. Daurelle, "My Vocation," 48–52.

WHAT WAS JESUS' INTENTION?

The many testimonies of Catholic women who feel called to the priesthood are sad indeed, especially when we study the facts.

Recent Popes, like Paul VI[2] and John-Paul II[3] have repeated the ban on women's ordination, basing it on Jesus' words at the Last Supper. "When Jesus said: 'Do this in memory of me!', he addressed the command to the apostles," they said. "Jesus only chose men to be apostles. Only men can receive priestly ordination."

A careful scrutiny of the text presents a different picture. The Last Supper was a paschal meal for Jesus and the whole family had to be invited to take part in it. We can be sure that Jesus' mother Mary and other women were present on that occasion.

The Catholic Church has always accepted that when Jesus stated: "Take this bread and eat!", he invited all disciples, including women to communion. Why then would his "Do this in memory of me!", be a commission restricted to the apostles only?

Have church leaders forgotten the real historical grounds for excluding women from the priestly ministry? The early Church was dominated by Greek and Roman culture. For the Greeks women were inferior by nature. Romans put women firmly under control of their fathers or husbands. Women could not hold official positions of authority. Their testimony was invalid in court.

And medieval St Thomas Aquinas, hailed by the same Popes as the leading Doctor of Orthodox Doctrine, spelled it out neatly in his *Summa Theologica* (1268–1273).

> "The image of God is found in man in a special way, and not in woman: for man is the beginning and end of woman; as God is the beginning and end of every creature . . . For man is not of woman, but woman of man; and man was not created for woman, but woman for man."[4]
>
> "(In creation) man is ordered to a still nobler vital action, and that is intellectual operation . . . woman is naturally

2. Paul VI, *Inter Insigniores*, §27.

3. John Paul II, *Ordinatio Sacerdotalis*, §1–4.

4. Aquinas, *Summa Theologica*, I qu. 92, art. 2 & I qu. 93, art. 4 ad 1.

subject to man, because in man the discretion of reason predominates."[5]

"(To the question: why are some humans born as women?) "With regard to the specific cause [i.e., *the action of the male semen*], a female is deficient and unintentionally caused. For the active power of the semen always seeks to produce a thing completely like itself, something male. So if a female is produced, this must be because the semen is weak or because the material [*provided by the female parent*] is unsuitable, or because of the action of some external factor such as the winds from the south which make the atmosphere humid. But with regard to general Nature, the female is not accidentally caused but is intended by Nature for the work of generation. Now the intentions of Nature come from God, who is its author. This is why, when he created Nature, he made not only the male but also the female."[6]

"The male sex is required for receiving Orders . . . even though a woman were made the object of all that is done in conferring Orders, she would not receive Orders, for since a sacrament is *a sign*, not only the thing, but *the signification* of the thing, is required in all sacramental actions. Accordingly, since it is not possible in the female sex to signify eminence of degree, for a woman is in the state of subjection, it follows that she cannot receive the sacrament of Order . . ."[7]

Do we need to say more?

QUESTIONS

1. Have you, in your personal experience, come across remnants of the prejudices that derive from Greek, Roman and medieval scholars? Were they dealt with successfully, or did they still cause damage?

5. Aquinas, *Summa Theologica*, I qu. 92, art. 1, ad 2.
6. Aquinas, *Summa Theologica*, I qu. 92, art 1, ad 1.
7. Aquinas, *Summa Theologica Suppl.*, qu. 39 art. 1.

2. What is your opinion about Jesus' mind? Did he, when conferring spiritual power on his successors in the ministry, intend to include or exclude women?

3. Is there anything you can do about the present situation in the Church?

10

The authority of teachers

Then Jesus spoke to the crowds and to his disciples: "The scribes and the Pharisees sit on the seat of Moses. So practice and observe everything they tell you." (Matt 23:1–3)

"Yes, I have researched your family tree, Father. Well, here it is!"

WHEN I STUDIED THEOLOGY at a Major Seminary in London in the late 1950's, one of our professors was a Dutch priest, Daan Duivesteijn. We called him 'Duivy'. He was a fierce defender of 'the faith'.

One day Duivy railed against evolutionists. "They find a jaw-bone of an ape," he said mockingly, "then construct a whole imaginary body around it and claimed it was a pre-human!" He then quoted Pope Pius XII's encyclical *Humani Generis* (1950) which allowed discussion on evolution, but then declared: "The Catholic faith obliges us to hold that souls are immediately created by God ... Some theologians rashly transgress the liberty of discussion, when they act as if the origin of the human body from pre-existing and living matter were already completely certain and proved by the facts which have been discovered up to now and by reasoning on those facts, and as if there were nothing in the sources of divine revelation which demands the greatest moderation and caution in this question."[1]

We knew Duivy was wrong. I myself had picked up many outstanding works on evolution that reported extensively on the scientific research that underpinned evolution. A study by Ralph von Koenigswald on hominids and apes convinced me that a common ancestor was undeniable. Von Koenigswald proved that of 1065 anatomical features, human beings share 396 with chimpanzees, 385 with gorillas and 354 with orangutans.

As Duivy was talking, a picture was passed down the lecture hall from one row of students to the next. It showed a chimpanzee, under which someone had scribbled: "Looks just like Duivy, doesn't it?"

Almost a hundred years after Darwin's *The Origin of Species*, the official Church was still not really listening to what scholars were saying ...

THE SCRIBES

In Jesus' days the scribes were teachers who studied and explained the Old Testament Law. Their origin can be traced back to the 4th century BC when, after exile, a number of Jews had returned to Jerusalem. They realised that they needed to observe the Law more

---

1. Pius XII, *Humani Generis*, §25.

diligently. One of them called Ezra took the initiative. He established a school of students. And when the time was ripe he started his public teaching sessions: "Ezra stood upon a pulpit of wood (surrounded by disciples) . . . He read out the book of the Law of Moses . . . He (and his disciples) made the people understand the law . . . They proclaimed the book of the law distinctly, made sense of it, caused the people to understand the reading" (Neh 8:4–8).

Jesus often argued with the scribes:

- when they questioned his power: "Who can forgive sins but God alone?" (Luke 5:21–28);

- when they asked him for a sign (Matt 12:38–42);

- when they accused Jesus of driving out demons 'by Beelzebul, the prince of demons' (Mark 3:22–30).

Jesus strongly criticised the scribes of his time: for their hypocrisy, for their putting heavy burdens on people's shoulders they were not willing to carry themselves, for taken seats of honour at banquets and in synagogues (Matt 23:1–7).

He even said: "Don't call yourself 'Rabbi', for you have one Teacher, and you are all brothers. Do not call anyone on earth 'father', for you have one Father who is in heaven. Nor call yourselves instructors, for you have one instructor, the Messiah." Then Jesus explains why they should avoid such titles—namely: "those who exalt themselves will be humbled" (Matt 23:8–12). But did Jesus thereby deny *the function* of the scribe or *the authority* of the teacher? He did not.

Jesus clearly taught: "The teachers of the law and the Pharisees sit upon Moses' seat. So you must be careful to do everything they tell you." (Matt 23:2–3).

Archaeologists have found synagogues in Palestine which featured a stone chair carved from a single stone of basalt that faced Jerusalem. This, apparently, was the 'seat of Moses'. Rabbis made authoritative pronouncements from the Hebrew Scriptures while sitting in this chair. Those who sat upon the seat of Moses clearly inherited Moses' authority. Jesus admits that authority. He urges people to accept what they teach. Remember: scribes were not priests.

In the Early Church the charism of teaching was acknowledged as a specific function distinct from the ordained ministry. Paul lists 'first of all apostles, secondly prophets, thirdly teachers, then workers of miracles, also those having gifts of healing, those able to help others, those with gifts of administration' (1 Cor 12: 27–28).

Ordination to the priesthood or the episcopacy does not impart theological knowledge, in spite of bishops presumptuously claiming the title of 'Doctor of Divinity'. This also applies to popes. They should therefore listen to the advice offered by scholars who have studied Sacred Scripture and other sources of doctrine in depth.

Though guided by the Spirit in their own way, priests or bishops do not enjoy the specific insights acquired by biologists, psychologists, sociologists and other academics. These too are guided by the Spirit.

QUESTIONS

1. Recent teachings by popes prohibit the use of artificial contraception in family planning, ban the ordination of women and condemn same-sex unions, in spite of strong contradictions by Catholic scholars. Has this impacted your own life or that of people you know? What has been your response?

2. What do you think of the 'oath of loyalty' to papal teaching imposed on scholars as a condition to them acquiring teaching posts in seminaries, colleges and universities? Do you believe this is a correct policy to safeguard our Catholic faith?

3. Jesus promised he would continue to speak to us through his Spirit? What is your own thought? Did Jesus' Spirit reveal his mind more through concerned scholars than in the prohibitions of those recent popes?

4. Is there anything you can do about it?

11

The authority of prophets

"Truly I tell you, among those born of women there has not risen anyone greater than John the Baptist; yet whoever is least in the kingdom of heaven is greater than he." (Matt 11:10–11)

"Do not worry about what to say or how to say it. At that time you will be given what to say, for it will not be you speaking, but the Spirit of your Father speaking through you." (Matt 10:17–20)

"Don't knock out your pharmacist, Father! You need him for your gout."

ON ONE OF MY lecture tours I was the guest of the bishop of a small missionary diocese in the North of India. He told me an interesting story. I will recount it with some small alterations for the sake of anonymity. The substance is true.

"Every Christmas we had a huge problem," the bishop told me. "The local Shah and his extended family would turn up for Christmas mass in the cathedral, occupying the first five rows of benches on every side. As Muslims, they too wanted to celebrate Christ's birth. But our own Christians, mainly from poor low-class backgrounds, were pushed aside at that most important feast every year. I did not know what to do—till I read the legend of cunning painter Fernando. Do you know it?"

"No," I said.

"Well, a Spanish king was blind in one eye and lame in one leg. One day, the king announced that he was looking for an artist who would paint an elegant portrait of himself. None of the established painters dared to consider the job as it was infeasible for them to paint an angelic portrait of a physically disabled man. However, Fernando agreed and painted a classic picture of the king—a painting so phenomenal that it earned admiration. He painted the king hunting aiming at a deer, targeting with one eye closed and one leg bent. I concluded that I too needed to be cunning. I discussed this with my secretary. 'I need to give the Shah a clever excuse', I told him.."

"He advised me against it. 'No', he said. 'Why not be straightforward? Just explain your predicament to the Shah'. Well, after some thinking I decided to follow his prophetic advice. Yes, my secretary was proved right. The Shah understood. We agreed to have a shared Christian-Muslim celebration of Jesus' birth in the afternoon of every Christmas day."

PROPHETS

Let us start by realising that we miss the point if we think that a prophet is someone who foretells the future. No, in the biblical understanding of the term, a prophet speaks authoritatively

43

in God's name. When God concluded a covenant with the Jewish people, three distinct ministries emerged: priests who sacrificed in the temple, kings who governed and prophets who spoke messages in God's name. The role played by prophets is well illustrated in the Old Testament books recording their sayings: the four major and twelve minor prophets. In Hebrew a prophet was called a 'Navi' probably meaning a person in whom fire bubbles up.

It is worth noting also that these prophets came from all kinds of social backgrounds. Isaiah worked at the royal court in Jerusalem. Jeremiah and Ezekiel served in the temple as priests. Amos herded a flock of sheep. Hosea was probably a businessman. Nehemiah, a Hebrew exile, worked for the king of Persia. Yes, these were ordinary people. Seeing what was wrong in their day and age, they would feel God's anger bubble up in them. Then, inspired by God's Spirit, they would manifest God's will.

Jesus accepted the authority of the Old Testament prophets. In his preaching he often referred to them in general terms (Luke 6:23; 11:47; Matt 13:17). But he also mentioned them by name: for instance Elijah (Luke 4:25–26), Elisha (Luke 4:27), Isaiah (Matt 12:17) and Jonah (Matt 12:39).

PROPHETS IN JESUS' OWN TIME

Jesus obviously regarded John the Baptist a true prophet. On one occasion he stated clearly: "What did you go out to see? A prophet? Yes, I tell you, and more than a prophet . . . Truly I tell you, among those born of women there has not risen anyone greater than John the Baptist; yet whoever is least in the kingdom of heaven is greater than he" (Matt 11:9–11).

But notice that last phrase: "whoever is least in the kingdom of heaven is greater than John the Baptist" (Matt 11:11). It means that all Jesus' followers, everyone baptised in his name, in principle possesses the gift of prophecy.

He also says this clearly in this statement: "You will be handed over to the local councils and be flogged in the synagogues. On my account you will be brought before governors and kings as witnesses to them and to the Gentiles. But when they arrest you, do not worry about what to say or how to say it. At that time you will be given what to say, for it will not be you speaking, but the Spirit of your Father speaking through you" (Matt 10:17–20).

And the Spirit will speak through God's people not only in such dramatic moments as when interrogated in captivity. God's Spirit may speak when, in ethical or religious matters, members of the faithful give their honest advice. Jesus too heard his Father's Spirit in what people said to him. It is remarkable to note how often Jesus allowed himself to be led by suggestions made by others.

- At Cana Jesus had not intended to do a miracle. "My hour has not yet come" (John 2:4). Yet he performed the miracle because his mother asked him to do so.

- It was actually Andrew who first introduced Simon Peter to Jesus. Jesus rewarded Andrew's initiative by accepting Peter as one of the apostles.

- Jesus gave in to Nicodemus who wanted to speak to him at night.

- He said "yes" to the Samaritans of Sychar when they requested him to stay for some days in their city.

The gift of prophecy continues to operate in our own time. Of course, discernment is required. Some honest persons may give advice which on careful examination proves to be misguided. But may a multiplicity of voices be so easily dismissed? If, for instance, as polls indicate, voices calling for the priestly ordination of women are supported by more than 70% of Catholics in major countries,[1] should they not be taken seriously?

QUESTIONS

1. What is your experience with regard to prophetic voices in the Church? Have you been aware of them? Were they

---

1. Wijngaards, *Ordination of Women*, 44–47.

listened to, or not? Did you get the impression church leaders act as if the gift of prophecy has been lost in our time? Or has your experience been more positive?

2. How do you personally think Jesus would appraise the present state of affairs?

3. Is there anything you can do to boost the chance of prophecies being listened to?

12

The authority of the community

"If your brother sins against you, go and tell him his fault, between you and him alone. If he listens, to you, you have gained your brother. But if he does not listen, take one or two others along with you, that every word may be confirmed by the evidence of two or three witnesses. If he refuses to listen to them, tell it to the community; and if he refuses to listen even to the community, let him be to you as a gentile and a tax collector." (Matt 18: 15–18)

"Why are you here?" "I hacked my way into church to attend Mass."

I REMEMBER LIKE THE day of yesterday the conflict that took place in the Catholic village of Huissen, the Netherlands, in the early 1950's. I was just approaching the end of my high school studies.

As it happened, there were two Catholic churches in the village. One was the large chapel of a Dominican monastery already founded in 1858, which had originally served the Catholic community as a parish headquarters. Then there was the new diocesan church which the archbishop of Utrecht established to take over the parish. It was looked after by diocesan clergy.

The problem was that the majority of Catholics preferred to attend Mass in the Dominican church. They were used to it. They also liked the singing of the choir, the sermons and the pastoral care provided there. So, while on every Sunday the Dominican chapel was filled to the brim, services in the diocesan church were poorly attended. The secular clergy complained to the archbishop.

The later Cardinal Alfrink, then only coadjutor bishop of Utrecht archdiocese, took charge. Without consulting the laity, he decided that the Dominican chapel should be closed on Sundays. When the prior stated that he could not stop people from entering the church doors, Alfrink ordered that those doors be barred with padlocks.

The local people were furious. On Sunday the 6th of January 1952 a huge crowd of up to a thousand people stormed the Dominican chapel. Some took the lead. Swinging axes they cut off the padlocks and hacked their way into the church. They attended Mass in what they considered their own place. For remember, in the Netherlands, the building of churches was always paid for by the conscientious contributions of the local community.

The matter was only resolved three years later through a compromise. The chapel was closed but the local parish was entrusted to the Dominicans.

DECISIONS TAKEN BY THE COMMUNITY

In the Hellenistic world of Jesus' times, the *ekklesia*, that is the local community, played an important part. Leaders of cities had to

THE AUTHORITY OF THE COMMUNITY

discuss their policies with the *ekklesia* of the town, a gathering in which all free citizens could take part. The *ekklesia* took decisions. The Early Church followed this pattern. Before selecting and ordaining the seven deacons, the apostles "summoned the whole groups of disciples" and explained their plan. The decisions were taken by the whole community, the 'assembly', though the laying on of hands was done by the apostles (Acts 7:5–6). Inspired by a vision Peter had, he admitted the pagan Cornelius to baptism, but he had to justify himself before the assembly (Acts 11: 1–18). It was the assembly at Antioch that sent Paul and Barnabas on their missionary journey (Acts 13: 1–3) and that received their first report (Acts 14:26–27).

If we keep this background in mind, we will understand the significance of the two Matthean passages where the word "community" (*ekklesia*) occurs. It is quite certain that Jesus did not employ the Greek term *'ekklesia'*. This for two reasons: Jesus spoke Aramaic, and *'ekklesia'*, church assembly, was a reality which only came about at Pentecost (Acts 2:44–47). The community was probably called *'ekklesia'* only later on, under the influence of Greek speaking converts. Jesus probably used the Aramaic term 'qahal'.

Remember also that the evangelists at times attribute to Jesus phrases that could only have arisen later.

- Luke makes Jesus say that we should take up our cross 'daily' when following Jesus (Luke 9:23). This is what Luke under inspiration understood Jesus meant. When Jesus was alive, the addition of 'daily' would have been unintelligible for his audience. For the taking up of the cross was one final event leading to crucifixion (cf. Mark 8:34).

- The evangelist Mark makes Jesus promise a special reward for giving a cup of water to those 'who bear the name of Christ' (Mark 9:41). But we know that it was more than twelve years later, at Antioch, that the disciples were first called after Christ (Acts 11:26). The substance of Jesus' teaching was retained, but the terminology updated.

We may be sure, therefore, that Matthew 18:15–17 reflects the mind of Jesus, even though some of the expressions may reflect the usage of the early church.

THE ROLE OF THE COMMUNITY IN JESUS' EYES

The case discussed in Matthew 18:15–17 is an instructive one. Jesus speaks of some quarrel between two disciples and presupposes that the other person is at fault. Elsewhere Jesus had already insisted that a quarrel should be settled before offering a sacrifice: "first go and reconcile yourself" (Matt 5:24). Here more detailed suggestions are given. If a personal effort at reconciliation proves fruitless, the help of some others will have to be called in. As a last resort, the matter should be brought to the community which will have an authoritative voice (Matt 18:17). Notice how it is the whole assembly, and not one or two elders, who have the last word: "If he refuses to listen to the community let him be to you as a pagan" (Matt 18:17). Of course, Christ's minister has a special function within the community, yet it is the whole community that should take the decision according to Jesus' directive.

Christ is present to us in more than one way. He comes to us in the person of his minister. "Who receives you, receives me" (Matt 10:40). But Christ also makes himself present to us through the community of believers.

- "Where two or three meet in my name, I shall be there with them" (Matt 18:20).

- Christ is present in the community by its common prayer: "If two of you on earth agree to ask anything at all" (Matt 18:19).

- He is present by the bond of unity: "Father, may they be one in us. . . so that the world may believe it was you who sent me" (John 17:21).

- Christ is present by decisions taken by the whole community as a group : "Whatever you (plural !) will bind on earth, shall be bound in heaven" (Matt 18:18).

Christ shines forth through the community as priest, prophet and king. The whole community partakes in this.

Fidelity to Christ's teaching requires that both aspects of the church are kept intact: the authority of the ministers and the authority of the community. An assembly without Christ's minister, like a Council without Pope, or a diocese without bishop, cannot stand as a community of Christ. But the minister cannot replace the community. A pope cannot overrule a General Council. A bishop may not ignore his diocesan faithful.

QUESTIONS

1. The Second Vatican Council stressed the importance of church community: the collegiality of the bishops[1], the role of bishops' conferences[2] and the need of pastoral councils on all levels.[3] What is your experience about this? Has Vatican II been implemented?

2. Do you agree that decisions by pastoral councils should only be *consultative* as Pope Paul VI laid down in church law,[4] that means: just advisory? Or should they be *deliberative* regarding some matters, that is: binding?

3. What do you personally think is Jesus' position on the matter?

4. Is there anything you can do to bolster the role of the community in the Church?

1. Vatican II, "Lumen Gentium §22." in Flannery, *Vatican Council II*, 374–75.

2. Vatican II, "Christus Dominus §36–8." in Flannery, *Vatican Council II*, 586–87.

3. Vatican II, "Christus Dominus §27." in Flannery, *Vatican Council II*, 579–80.

4. Canon Law Society, *The Code of Canon Law*, canon 536.

13

The authority of the Catholic 'sense of faith'

"People can be forgiven any sin and any evil thing they say: but whoever says evil things against the Holy Spirit will not be forgiven. Anyone who says something about the Son of Man will be forgiven; but whoever says something against the Holy Spirit will not be forgiven, now or ever." (Mathew 12:31–32)

"My sense of faith tells me that you can find me somewhere to sleep."

I WAS BORN ON a hot steamy monsoon day in St Vincent de Paul Hospital at Surabaya, Indonesia, then still known as the Dutch East Indies. The date was Monday 30 September 1935. My parents were Dutch. My father served as headmaster of a primary school that had both Dutch speaking and Malay speaking sections.

When my mother had been wheeled back from the delivery room to the ward, a clash occurred with parish authorities. The details of the event were duly recorded in my family records. My parents were devout Catholics and daily communicants whenever possible. So my mother requested to be brought holy communion next day as was her custom.

"Out of the question!," the religious sister in the hospital stated, refusing to put her on the list for holy communion. "You have not been *churched*!"

Those were the days when 'churching' was still practised by Catholics in many countries. This atrocious custom was the outcome of ancient fears surrounding childbirth joined to medieval prejudice based on Leviticus 12:2–8. After childbirth a woman was deemed unclean. A young mum would present herself forty days after delivery at the church door with a lighted candle in one hand and an offering in the other. Only when a priest had blessed her, thus purifying her from all menstrual stain, could she again participate in the eucharist. It also meant that a mother was prevented from attending the baptism of her newborn child which took place in church soon after birth.

My mother who had seen her own mum who had nine children being churched many a time, had sworn that she herself would never submit to the rite.

"I don't need to be churched," she asserted.

"But you're unclean. You don't want to disgrace the Blessed Sacrament do you?"

"I've just done the most wonderful thing in my life and given birth to a child," my mother retorted. "Why would I need to be cleansed?"

The Sister did not want to give in. Nor did my mother. She insisted that the parish priest be called. Father Jan Zoetmuller of

Sacred Heart Parish dutifully arrived. More words followed as he too tried to persuade her. To no avail. My mother insisted that he bring her communion as before.

Next morning on Tuesday 1 October 1935 my mother received holy communion as usual. Afterwards she was present when the parish priest baptised me in the chapel of the hospital.

The point of the story is that my mother had not been theologically trained. No one had told her that 'churching' was not right. She simply *knew* it was wrong. She knew it from the deep 'sense of faith' she carried in her heart. And she was proved right. After the Second Vatican Council 'churching' has been totally abolished.

THE 'SENSE OF FAITH'

How do we know what truly belongs to our Catholic faith? Is it only what priests, bishops, the pope tell us? No. An important source lies in our hearts and minds. In the past it has been called the 'sense of faith', the 'sense of the faithful', the 'Gospel in the heart', the 'Catholic sense', the 'ecclesiastical spirit', the 'sense of the church', or sometimes the 'consensus of the church', remembering that in these last expressions 'church' stands for the whole community of believers. Tradition has always stressed the crucial role which the 'sense of faith' plays in the life of the church. For it is alive and aware.

The sense of faith in our hearts does not just carry a bundle of old truths. Under guidance of the Spirit it tests new developments and it assesses their value. Our minds come across new problems and fresh possibilities, which makes our faith blossom with an enriched vision. It leads to reaction to old truths, adaptation, growth and fruitfulness. This makes Christian Tradition a *living* tradition, alive because it opens up to wider horizons while facing questions that need answering. The sense of faith is the people of God's awareness, an ever renewed awareness.

The Second Vatican Council teaches that this 'sense of faith' lies at the root of infallibility/inerrancy:

"The body of the faithful as a whole, anointed as they are by the Holy One (cf. 1 John 2:20.27), cannot err in matters of belief. Thanks to a supernatural *sense of the faith* which characterizes the People as a whole, it manifests this unerring quality when 'from the bishops down to the last member of the laity', it shows universal agreement in matters of faith and morals. For, by this *sense of faith* which is aroused and sustained by the Spirit of truth, God's People accepts not the word of human beings, but the very Word of God (cf. 1 Thessalonians 2:13). It clings without fail to the faith once delivered to the saints, penetrates it more deeply by accurate insights, and applies it more thoroughly to life."[1]

Some Vatican documents in recent decades have attempted to minimise the impact of the 'sense of faith'. They stipulate that the pope, bishops, priests must agree. They reject the value of polls. They list qualities a Catholic must possess before his or her 'sense of faith' counts. And, of course, it is true. Someone's 'sense of faith' can at times be misguided. But what about the danger of underrating it?

WHAT DID JESUS THINK ABOUT IT?

All Jesus' preaching and miracles were a manifestation of the Spirit. "The Spirit of God is upon me. The Spirit has anointed me to preach the good news to the poor. The Spirit has sent me to proclaim liberty to the captives" (Luke 4:18). Notice that Jesus says he was *anointed* by God's Spirit. Anointment was a ritual to give someone an official position, like a priest or a king.

When Jesus talks to Nicodemus, he explains to him that through baptism a person is born again, the second birth being not of an earthly mother but of the Spirit. "Truly I tell you, no one can enter the kingdom of God unless they are born of water and the Spirit. Flesh gives birth to flesh, but the Spirit gives birth to Spirit. You should not be surprised at my saying, 'You must be born

---

1. Vatican II, "Lumen Gentium §12," in Flannery, *Vatican Council II*, 363.

again.' The wind blows wherever it pleases. You hear its sound, but you cannot tell where it comes from or where it is going. So it is with everyone born of the Spirit" (John 3:5-8).

At the Last Supper Jesus confirms this again: "I will ask the Father and he will give you another helper, the Spirit of Truth to remain with you forever. The world did not receive the Spirit, because it cannot see the Spirit and know the Spirit. But you know the Spirit, for the Spirit remains with you and lives in you" (John 14:16-17).

It is through the Spirit that everyone of the faithful has that deep sense of faith by which he or she knows what is in line with what Jesus taught, with the Father's kingdom of love which he came to bring about.

The first letter of John expresses very clearly that this results in a degree of inerrancy: "As for you, the anointing you received from him remains in you and you do not need anyone to teach you. But just as his true and genuine anointing teaches you all about things, so remain in him as you have been taught" (1 John 2:27).

QUESTIONS

1. What is your experience with regard to the presence of the 'sense of faith' in the Church? Do you feel that the 'teaching authority' of the Church in our time in actual fact ignores the 'sense of faith'? Or do you feel the opposite: that the 'sense of faith' is fully taken into account?

2. Do you believe Jesus would share your assessment of the situation?

3. If anything needs mending, what can you personally do about it?

14

Latent spiritual authority shared by all

Jesus said to the Apostle John: "Do not stop the man who is casting out devils in my name!! For the one who is not against you is for you." (Luke 9:49–50)

"Don't worry! If he gets mauled by the lion, I can hear his last confession."

In 1991 I visited Rio de Janeiro, Brazil, in the context of a video production. We were filming a story that would become part of the *Walking on Water* series of videos for adult faith formation.

I was staying in a monastery. There I met a religious sister whom I shall call 'Amelia'. She ministered as a hospital chaplain and she talked to me about her work. "At times I hear a patient's confession and forgive their sins," she told me.

"Great!," I said. "But—what does your bishop think about it?"

"He agrees," she said. "Well, it started like this. One day I was on the emergency ward of a large hospital when a young man was carried in. His motorbike had collided with a car. He had broken both legs and, apparently, he also suffered from internal bleeding in the stomach area. A nurse told me they did not expect him to last long . . ."

"I approached his bed. When he saw me, he clenched my hand and whispered: 'I need to go to confession.'"

"I was in shock. I realised that I would never be able to call a priest in time. What should I do? Then I remembered that in the past even ordinary Christians had heard the confession of other people . . . So I took a bold decision. 'I can hear your confession', I told him. He trusted me. I heard his confession and gave him absolution. Then I handed him holy communion which I always carry with me."

"Marvellous!," I said. "And what about your bishop?"

"Yes, that was my worry too. Had I done the right thing? So I explained to our local auxiliary bishop what I had done. He is an elderly man with a lot of experience. 'Leave it to me', he said. 'I must consult some people'. When I met him again after a few days, he said: 'You've done the right thing. Go ahead. Hear your patients' confessions when there is an urgent need.' And that is what I am doing."

SPIRITUAL POWER OF THE NON-ORDAINED?

The practice of the sacrament of penance has gone through a long and convoluted history. During the first few centuries after Christ, the forgiveness of sins was not restricted to bishops or priests. "Confess your sins one to another," the Apostle James prescribed (Jas 5:16).

Tradition recounts that Christians locked up in prison during the Roman persecutions would hear each other's confession. And even though by the early Middle Ages, absolution of sins was generally reserved to priests, knights wounded in battle during the crusades would confess their sins to comrades when no priest was present. The formula of absolution used was: "I absolve you from your sins with such power as God has given me."

Outside cultural factors muddled the picture. The problem is that, according to the Roman mindset, sins were not so much considered an offence against God, but an offence against law. This was reinforced by feudal thinking in the Middle Ages.

What did Jesus think about it?

DID JESUS RESTRICT AUTHORITY TO ORDAINED MINISTERS?

There is no doubt about the fact that Jesus designated the twelve apostles to a special ministry with specific spiritual powers. The early church, right from Jesus' death and resurrection, followed his example. They established 'elders' in each community, 'presbyters' = 'priests', and overseers/'episcopoi' = 'bishops', to coordinate larger areas. These ministers exercised spiritual authority. But was that authority restricted to them alone? Had that been Jesus' intention?

No, it had not. For instance, the first power Jesus gave to the Twelve was to drive out demons. "He gave them authority over unclean demons, to cast them out and heal every disease" (Matt 10:1). But when the Apostle John complains to Jesus that an ordinary disciple is casting out demons in Jesus' name, Jesus replies: "Do not stop him!! For the one who is not against you is for you" (Luke 9:49–50). In other words: the fact that the casting out of demons was a power specifically entrusted to the Twelve did not imply that other disciples did not inherently have that same power.

With regard to the forgiveness of sins, notice that ordinary disciples were present too when Jesus after the resurrection explicitly conferred that power. After mentioning Mary Magdalene explicitly (John 20:18), the text says: "On the evening of that first day of the week, when the disciples were together, with the doors locked for fear of the Jewish leaders, Jesus came and stood among them and said, 'Peace be with you!'" (John 20:19) It is not stated that his following words: "If you forgive anyone's sins, their sins are forgiven" was only spoken to the twelve (John 20:21–23). Everyone was somehow included. In the special passage that follows, Thomas is indicated as "also known as Didymus, one of the twelve, who had not been with the disciples when Jesus came" (John 20:24).

The same applies to presiding at the Eucharist. When Jesus at the Last Supper said "Do this in memory of me," other disciples were present. For it was his paschal meal when close family and friends, also women, had to take part (Luke 22:15). It is also implied in the fact that "Eat this!"—"Drink this!" has always been understood to be addressed to all the faithful. St Paul too links consecration and communion in the command 'Do this in memory of me'. "The Lord Jesus broke the bread and said, 'This is my body, which is for you; do this in remembrance of me'. In the same way, after supper he took the cup, saying, 'This cup is the new covenant in my blood; do this, whenever you drink it, in remembrance of me'" (1 Cor 11:24–25)

This means: Jesus addressed "Do this in memory of me" to all disciples. In principle all are empowered to preside at the eucharist. Yes, normally 'elders' or 'overseers' will preside, but if they are not present, any competent member of the community can, and should, fulfil that function.

QUESTIONS

1. What are your thoughts about all this? Should church leaders inform the faithful that, in special circumstances when no priest is present, any competent member of the community can preside at the Eucharist? Or would that go too far in your view?

2. And what about chaplains in hospitals and prisons? Should they not be routinely taught that, in special circumstances,

they too can hear confessions and absolve people from their sins? Or do you think the opposite?

3. Have you had personal experiences that involved such special circumstances?

4. What can you do to improve awareness of the latent spiritual powers of all the faithful?

15

No superior dignity

"The teachers of the law and the pharisees love the best places at feasts and the reserved seats in the meeting houses. They love to be greeted with respect in the marketplaces and have people call them 'teacher'. You must not be called 'teacher', for you are all brothers and sisters of one another and have only one Teacher. And you must not call anyone here on earth 'father' for you have only the one Father in heaven. Nor should you be called 'leader' because your one and only leader is the Christ." (Matt 23:6–10)

© Wijngaards Institute

"What do you mean you've lost your divine status?"

You will not believe what I am going to tell you, but it happened. It was the 1960s in the Flemish part of Belgium.

A friend of mine worked on the staff of a seminary for future priests. Now you must know that Catholics in Belgium, just as in the South of the Netherlands at the time, were very devout. They were committed churchgoers. They also had a very high regard for priests.

Most people were local farmers of small properties, not rich by any means. Stables for cows and pigs adjoined a farmer's house, as well a primitive toilet. The home itself would have an upper floor with bedrooms, and downstairs a kitchen and daily living room. It also usually had, near the front door, a small specially decorated 'upper' reception room. It was there that a priest would be received during his visit, to keep him away from the smell of the stables and the latrine.

My friend, lecturer in the seminary, spoke about the sometimes exaggerated esteem for priests. And he gave me one example.

Some weeks previously a couple from a local farm had visited the seminary. They were the parents of one of the students.

"I showed them the various places in the seminary," my friend said. "The chapel, the classrooms, the study room, the refectory, the recreation hall, etc. Then we came to the area with showers, latrines, toilets. The farmer had a good look round with some surprise on his face. Then he turned to me, shaking his head, and said: 'Yes . . . Of course. Priests too need to go to the toilet. . . .' As if he had not realised before that we priests too are human beings like everyone else."

This may seem an extreme story. The truth is that in many countries priests have been put on a pedestal. One of the consequences has been that some candidates applied—and perhaps still apply—to become priests in order to achieve that higher status.

A PRIVILEGED SOCIAL CLASS?

The Christian Middle Ages flourished as a feudalistic society. The community could roughly be divided into three groups: nobility, craftsmen and dependents, that meant often: slaves. People were considered to belong to one of these social statuses because they had been born into them. Or, to put it sociologically, they belonged to their status by *ascription*. A nobleman even though he was poor and dressed in rags, retained the respect due to a nobleman.

Owing to the prestige which the Church enjoyed in those centuries, the clergy were considered part of or parallel to the nobility. Most vocations would come from this group and becoming a priest or religious was not therefore considered a loss of status. A clergyman was respected simply because he was a clergyman, just as a nobleman was respected because he belonged to the nobility. This was also enshrined in church law.

The Church borrowed from the nobility many of the status symbols that now characterize the clergy. Canon Law enshrined customs that sought to underline the higher social status of the clergy. Examples are: the distinctive dress, the respectful form of address, the precedence to be given inside and outside of the church and the privilege of immunity.

Such status symbols were carefully graded according to hierarchical rank. A bishop was supposed to wear more purple than an ordinary *monsignore*. Whereas a bishop was called 'My Lord' (corresponding to the rank of a Baron), an archbishop was addressed as 'Your Grace' (the title reserved to Dukes) and a cardinal as 'Your Eminence'.

Modern society has moved away from the concept of higher and lower classes among people. By law all persons are considered full-fledged citizens with equal rights and duties. Position in society is, at least theoretically, due to what one does and not to one's family background. People are respected by virtue of their professions: surgeons, engineers, journalists, lawyers or ministers of state. In contrast, the Church has clung, in practice, to defending a higher status for clerics.

WHAT DID CHRIST THINK ABOUT THIS?

At the time of Christ, the scribes and pharisees considered themselves a class apart. They looked down on the ordinary people whom they called "*am ha-ares*," that is, "the people of the land." Rabbinical writings have preserved instances of real contempt. "A man should be ready to sell all he possesses to marry the daughter of a scribe. He should never take a daughter of the common folk, for these are contemptible and their daughters an abomination." Scribes were not expected to mingle with such people even in every-day life. "A pharisee should not enter a house of the common folk as a guest, neither give them hospitality as their host."

In this way scribes and pharisees claimed for themselves a higher dignity, a greater interior worth, a superior social standing and even a greater sanctity in the eyes of God.

This was the situation which Jesus criticized. He did not condemn only the individual pride of some scribes and pharisees, but their whole attitude as a group. As a class they insisted on precedence both in the synagogues and at social functions. As a class they wanted to be recognized and acclaimed whenever they appeared in public. As a class they had reserved some titles to themselves which other people were not allowed to use. To bring out the higher dignity which they thought they possessed, they put themselves on a pedestal.

Christ did not want his future ministers to form a similar higher-status group. "For you are all brothers and sisters of one another." "For you have only one Father who is in heaven." "Because your one and only leader is the Christ" (Matt 23:6–10).

In his own behaviour Jesus himself lived up to the principle of accepting a common dignity for all people. When he was born, he was put in a manger as any other child of the ordinary people would have been in the same circumstances (Luke 2:6). Those invited to celebrate his birth were common shepherds (Luke 2:7–8). Jesus spent his early life in the very hum-drum hamlet called Nazareth (John 1:36). He was known as 'the carpenter's son' and his mother and relations were considered people like anybody else

(Matt 13:55–56). The pharisees were scandalized because Jesus moved freely with 'tax collectors and outcasts' (Matt 9:11).

The one thing Jesus never did was putting himself on a pedestal, even though as Son of God he could have done so.

> The Second Vatican Council re-affirmed the essentially equal dignity of all its members. "There is in Christ and in the church no inequality on the basis of race or nationality, social condition or sex. . . And, if by the will of Christ some are made teachers, dispensers of ministries, and shepherds on behalf of others, yet *all share a true equality* with regard to the dignity and to activity common to all the faithful for the bearing up of the body of Christ."[1]

QUESTIONS

1. Have you come across a claim to a 'higher status' for bishops or priests in your own life? How did this strike you: as odd or as the right thing?

2. Some people in the Church think that a loss of social status for ordained ministers necessarily implies a loss of authority. It is the traditional view. Do you agree with that?

3. Is it an old 'feudal' misunderstanding of the kind of authority Jesus was thinking about? Or is it the kind of thing Jesus would have wanted for our age?

4. Is there anything you can do about safeguarding the true authority of ordained ministers?

1. Vatican II, "Lumen Gentium §32," in Flannery, *Vatican Council II*, 389–90.

16

No immunity from secular law

"If anyone causes one of these little ones—those who believe in me—to stumble, it would be better for them to have a large millstone hung around their neck and to be drowned in the depths of the sea." (Matt 18:6)

© Wijngaards Institute

"You are a reckless driver, Father! If you retain your driving licence, how safe is my other leg?"

WE ARE ALL AWARE of the child abuse scandal in the Church. Under instructions from Rome, priests who had been involved in child abuse were not referred to secular criminal authorities.

I myself came across such a case. After I had spoken to a group of Catholic women campaigning for the ordination of women, one person, whom I shall call 'Dawn', approached me. We became good friends. We stayed in touch. On one occasion she told me her experience as a child.

"I'm an orphan," she said. "My father divorced my mother and went abroad. My mother died when I was twelve years old. I landed up in an orphanage managed by religious sisters. The sisters treated me well. I'm greatly indebted to them. But our spiritual director inflicted permanent damage."

"What did he do?," I asked.

"Well, he came to the orphanage once a week to hear our confessions. Remember this was the 1970's. If we needed to discuss any special problem, we could meet him in a small parlour nearby. Well, on one occasion he told me at the end of confession to meet him in the parlour afterwards."

"I don't know if I should go into details," she told me. "But I suppose it is relief for me to share my story. On that day I waited till all confessions were over. Then I joined him in the parlour. He locked the door from the inside keeping the key in the door, sat down and asked me to come closer. 'I want to see if you are healthy and OK', he said. Then he lifted my skirt, pulled down my panty and interfered with me . . . I froze. I was terrified. I didn't know what to do. But he said everything was alright. I didn't need to worry . . . This happened a couple of times. On the last occasion he tried to rape me. I cried, managed to open the door and ran out of the room."

"Didn't you tell anyone?," I asked.

"Yes, I finally did. When Mother Superior found me sobbing in the dormitory, she took me to her office. I told her what had happened. She was upset. She embraced me and said: 'I'll sort this out'. She did, in quite a dramatic way. I was sent to another orphanage far away from the priest."

"And what happened to him?"

"Nothing as far as I know. Years later when I had grown up and got my first job, I visited the original orphanage. I was told the priest was still the spiritual director. I don't know if he molested other girls . . ."

Dawn also confided to me that, on account of that early experience and her resulting dread of men, she had never been able to marry.

ACCOUNTABILITY

The horror of child abuse committed by some bishops and priests is now well recognised. The Catholic Church handled the crisis badly especially under Pope John Paul II. Reasons were a serious underestimation of the emotional damage done to the victims; the failure to understand that child abuse springs from deep psychological disorders that lead to re-offending; and the belief that avoiding scandal to the Church's reputation should outweigh other considerations.

But another, more destructive, reason lay in the old concept that clerics were exempt from secular law. It was laid down in the earliest medieval form of it in these words: "The dragging of a cleric before a civil judge is prohibited by the sacred canons and the external (= secular) laws, both in civil and in criminal cases."[1] It remained enshrined in Church Law until 1983.

And the principle of clerical exemption is closely linked to another erroneous concept: that ordained persons are somehow only accountable to their ecclesiastical superiors and to God.

CHRIST AND EXEMPTION
FROM SECULAR LAW

It is clear that Jesus would be very upset by child abuse. He clearly stated: "If any of you put a stumbling block before one of these little ones who believe in me, it would be better for you if a great millstone were fastened around your neck and you were drowned

1. "Decretum Gratiani ch.32 no 24," in Friedberg, *Corpus Iuris Canonici*, 121–22.

in the depth of the sea" (Matt 18:6). Notice the phrase: "if *any* of you." There is no room here for clerical immunity. It includes 'apostles' or whoever would claim rank among his disciples.

But what about exemption from secular law?

Well, Jesus taught that the Jews of his time should pay tax to their secular rulers, the Romans. Remember the incident. When the Pharisees and Herodians ask him about this, he said: "Show me the coin used for the tax." And when they brought him a denarius, he asked: "Whose head is this, and whose title?" They answered, "The emperor's." Then Jesus declared: "Well, then give to the emperor the things that are the emperor's, and to God the things that are God's" (Matt 22:19–21). This is all the more telling because the Romans were foreign intruders.

Another telling feature is that, when Jesus cured lepers, he always instructed them to subject themselves to the priests in Jerusalem who were in charge of checking whether someone was infected by leprosy or not. Keeping lepers isolated was crucially important in Jewish society at the time to prevent further infections. Those specialised priests were the officially appointed authority. To a leper in the Galilean hill country Jesus gives this order: "See that you don't tell anyone. But go, show yourself to the priest and offer the gift Moses commanded, as a testimony to them" (Matt 8:4). To the ten lepers on the border between Samaria and Galilee Jesus says: "Go and show yourself to the priests!" (Luke 17:14). Jesus did not consider them immune from the established law.

When Jesus stands trial before Pilate, he does not claim immunity from secular law. Pilate asks him: "Are you the king of the Jews?" Jesus replies: "My kingdom is not of this world. If it were, my servants would fight to prevent my arrest by the Jewish leaders. But my kingdom is from another place [= *is a different kind of kingdom*]" (John 18:33–36). Even though Jesus knew he was unjustly condemned to death, he did not deny Pilate's secular authority over himself.

QUESTIONS

1. In recent years the official position on clerical immunity has changed. What is your own experience in this regard? Did you witness church leaders cooperate fully with secular authorities investigating misbehaviour or crimes committed by ordained persons? Or did you still experience a tendency to protect bishops or priests 'for the good of the Church'?

2. Would Jesus have approved of what you saw in action?

3. If there are deficiencies, what can you do to rectify a wrong?

17

Not office bound

"Whatever house you enter, first say, 'Peace be to this house!' And if peaceful people live there, your peace will rest upon them. But if not, it will return to you. Remain in the same house, eating and drinking what they provide." (Luke 10:5–6)

"Hey Father! We haven't seen you here for at least twenty years!"

IN 1980 I TRAVELLED to the United States. As Vicar General of the Mill Hill Missionaries I had responsibility not only for the institutions we ran in the country, but also for retired missionaries who had volunteered to help out in parishes. In that context I visited Florida. One of our Dutch missionaries who was in his seventies and who had ministered to the Maoris in New Zealand, was now in charge of a large parish not far from Jacksonville.

Martien, as I will call the priest in question, told me at breakfast about the background of his parish. "The elderly form a large group, many having retired here from other US States because of the warmer climate. We also have a fair number of Hispanics."

"Great," I said. "Are you supported in your ministry?"

"Oh yes, I am! The parish council is very active. In fact, this morning we have a session of the core group. Would you like to participate?"

"Yes, I would," I replied.

At the meeting Martien introduced me to the various 'ministers'.

- A couple were in charge of visiting newcomers to the area, and if they were Catholics to take their details and provide information about parish services.

- A lady had special responsibility for the sick and for arranging holy communion to be brought to them by some dedicated parishioners.

- One, a teacher, oversaw the preparation classes for children and the lectures for teenagers getting ready for confirmation.

- Another female teacher helped coordinate instructions for persons wanting to become Catholic. This often happened in the context of preparation for marriage.

All of these ministers alerted Martien of people he would be well advised to go and see in person. On top of that, aided by his secretary in the parish office, Martien tried to maintain a regular schedule of visiting homes in the parish. "The Maoris have some wonderful sayings," Martien told me. "My strength is not me an individual, but me the community." "What is the most important thing in the world? People, people, people."

FOCUS IN PARISH MINISTRY

Parishes in today's world cannot do without some central structures, such as a church building, the priest's house with attached office and so on. But studies in recent decades on parish ministry in Europe and North America have revealed two distinct approaches.

One may be called **'parish-centre-focussed' ministry**. At the centre of the parish lie the church where the Sunday services are celebrated, the parish office, a parish hall and often a local Catholic school. The parish clergy and supporting staff aim at serving the people as well as they can from these central locations. Masses celebrated in the church on Sundays provide an opportunity for the clergy to address the faithful. Moreover, people are invited to events organised in the parish hall. Individual Catholics with problems are expected to meet the priest in the parish office.

But another kind of ministry is being rediscovered: a **'People-of-God-focussed' ministry**. In this approach, the clergy and ministers who help them are keenly aware that people live their lives outside the church. They live in their homes, in their places of work, in establishments such as clubs and pubs where they relax. So, while enjoying the support of the central structures, priests and other ministers spend as much time as possible meeting the faithful in their own living spaces.

WHAT WAS JESUS' APPROACH?

It is clear from the Gospels that Jesus acknowledged the need of various forms of organization to assist him and the other apostles in their mission.

- Jesus chose Judas Iscariot, one of the twelve apostles, to be in charge of the purse, the money bag (John 12:6).

- When Jesus and his band pass the town of Sychar in Samaria, Jesus remains at the well outside the town, but the apostles enter Sychar to buy food (John 4:8).

- Jesus and his apostles were also accompanied by a group of women "who ministered unto him providing their own contributions." Mentioned by name are Mary Magdalene, Joanna the wife of Herod's steward Chuza and Susanna (Luke 8:2–3).

- On the day before his passion Jesus sent Peter and John to prepare for the Last Supper. "Where do you want us to prepare for it?" they asked. He replied, "As you enter the city, a man carrying a jar of water will meet you. Follow him to the house that he enters, and say to the owner of the house, 'The Teacher asks: Where is the guest room, where I may eat the Passover with my disciples?' He will show you a large upper room, all furnished. Make preparations there." (Luke 22:7–13).

However, Jesus never focussed on structural organization. He focussed squarely on people. He used whatever convenient location he found to address the people.

On occasion he preached to people standing on the shore from a fishing boat (Luke 5:1–3). Or he would climb on a hill to speak to them (Matt 5:1–2). He preached in people's homes, like Peter's (Mark 2:1–5), in Tyre (Mark 7:24–26), a Pharisee's house (Luke 36–50) and Martha's home (Luke 10:38–42). He often preached to people he met on the road. He "preached in the synagogues of Galilee" (Luke 4:14–15). He also preached in the temple of Jerusalem (Mark 12:35; John 7:28). He preached to people in all their own places.

And when he sent out his apostles and disciples, he did not urge them to set up impressive structures. He told them to focus on people:

- The twelve—"Go to the lost sheep of Israel. Proclaim this message: 'The kingdom of heaven has come near.' Heal the sick, raise the dead, cleanse those who have leprosy, drive out demons" (Matt 10:6–8).

- The 72 disciples—"Whatever house you enter, first say, 'Peace be to this house!' And if peaceful people live there, your peace will rest upon them. But if not, it will return to you. Remain in the same house, eating and drinking what they provide, for the laborer deserves his wages. Do not go from house to house. Whenever you enter a town and they receive you, eat what is set before you. Heal the sick in it and say to them, 'The kingdom of God has come near to you.'" (Luke 10:5–9)

- And at the ascension—"Go and make disciples of all nations. Baptize them in the name of the Father and of the Son and of the Holy Spirit. And teach them to obey everything I have commanded you" (Matt 28:19–20).

QUESTIONS

1. What is your experience of ministry in the Church? Is it people focussed or parish-centre focussed? Do the clergy and other pastoral ministers interact with parishioners from a church building or parish office? Or do they go out and meet parishioners in their own homes and other living spaces?

2. How do you think Jesus would exercise that ministry?

3. Is there anything you can do to strengthen the right approach?

18

Not of this world!

"You know that the kings of the nations exercise authority over them, and their leaders rule over them. This, however, is not the way it shall be among you." (Matt 20:25–26)

"All [the Pharisees] do, they do for people to see. They broaden their phylacteries and lengthen their tassels. They love the places of honour at banquets, the chief seats in the synagogues." (Matt 23:5–6)

"Your Grace, if I cut off more hair your mitre may no longer fit!"

IN MY TRAVELS AROUND the world as Vicar General of Mill Hill I visited Catholic dioceses on all continents. I am still full of admiration for the excellent work done in all of them—through parishes, hospitals, clinics, schools, boarding houses and development projects. But at times I also witnessed truly ancient scenes.

When visiting the house of one archbishop whose name I shall not mention, I got to know 'the power of the episcopal ring'. The priest who introduced me to the archbishop whispered to me: "Do kiss his ring! It's essential!"

True enough. The archbishop held out his right hand for me to kiss his ring. It was of considerable size and sparkled in the tropical sunshine.

Later I accompanied the archbishop to one of his outstations in the diocese. It was quite a long trip and, when we arrived at our destination, the noontime heat was overwhelming. A welcoming party of the local priest, religious sisters and prominent laity had been waiting for our arrival in front of the priest's house.

The archbishop stepped out of his car. He allowed the priest to kiss his ring. But seeing the crowd anxious to do the same, he hesitated for a moment on what to do. He wiped his forehead and decided it was too hot to go round to many people. So he took the ring from his hand and, before entering the shade of the priest's house, ordered the ring to be passed round so that all would have a chance to kiss it.

Believe me, it truly happened.

REMNANTS OF FEUDAL POWER.

Jesus taught that authority in the Church should be different from that exercised by kings, the traditional secular rulers. But has the Church not failed to listen to that injunction?

To begin with, the Church has adopted for its ministers many symbols of secular authority. Just think of the way bishops are presented.

Fully attired in episcopal vestments, a bishop displays princely splendour derived from the early Middle Ages.

The bishop sits on a 'throne'.

He wears a mitre and holds the crozier, a ruler's staff.

Over his head a 'coat of arms' proclaims his right to dignity.

He is addressed with "My Lord," "Your Grace" or "Your Excellency"—graded titulature borrowed from feudalistic society.

Bishops wear an episcopal ring.

Since the Vatican Council, such a display of secular majesty is now being discouraged and most bishops are more careful displaying them. The fact remains that much in the exercise of papal and episcopal power derives from secular sources.

HOW DID JESUS DISPLAY HIMSELF?

He did not wear the linen *ephod*, the special apron worn by the high priest in Jerusalem, not even the *me'il*, the robe worn by ordinary Jewish priests. Nor did he indulge in any 'purple' dress, the colour reserved to high-ranking officials in the Roman world. He continued to use the tunic and mantle he had always worn when working as the 'carpenter', the handyman, in Nazareth.

Interpreting some instructions of the law—the *Torah*—literally, pious Jews in Jesus' days strapped small leather boxes with scripture texts to their left arm or forehead. They were known as *phylacteries*. They would also attach some dangling bits of blue thread, *tassels*, to the four corners of a man's garment. We don't know if Jesus wore them, but he chides the Pharisees for enlarging them so that people would admire their piety.

QUESTIONS

1. Since Vatican II much has improved in the Church. No longer is the Pope's palanquin surrounded by knights carrying imperial ostrich feathers as was done in the past. No longer do Cardinals drag a ten-meter red trail along the floor of the cathedral, as I still saw in pre-conciliar days. Much ostentation has been reduced.

2. But what is your experience of all this? Have you witnessed too much 'pomp' on display? Or did you find the toned-down symbols of episcopal or priestly 'status' are acceptable, or even helpful?

3. Do you think Jesus agrees with your assessment?

4. Is there personally anything you can do to strike the right balance?

19

No ministry to enjoy luxury

"Jesus summoned the twelve and began to send them out in pairs. He gave them authority over unclean spirits. And he instructed them that they should take nothing for their journey, except a mere staff—no bread, no bag, no money in their belt— but to wear sandals. And he added: 'Do not put on two tunics." (Mark 6:7–9)

"Tourists? Charge an entrance fee! They have the cash."

DURING MY MINISTRY IN India in the 1960s I enjoyed the privilege of staying in bishops' residences all over the country. Most bishops, I found, live in efficient, suitable accommodation. Depending on the needs of their diocese, they live in houses large enough to provide lodgings to immediate staff and visiting clergy. However, there are exceptions.

On a visit to the south of India I encountered a bishop's residence of truly majestic proportions. I had been instructed that on taking a rickshaw from the railway station, I should ask to be directed to 'Bishop's Palace'. And a palace it truly was.

After we had been let in through the wide entrance gate, we entered a blossoming front garden, luscious palm trees on both sides of the drive, peacocks strolling between flower beds.

The palace itself had two colossal wings. The outside was beautifully decorated with carved images. The ground floor provided spacious rooms: a meeting room, a dining room, a lounge, offices, an impressive kitchen area. Upstairs was the bishop's own apartment as well as rows of comfortable visitors' rooms. Throughout the building samples of local art were displayed: tapestry, statues, paintings and vases. Adjacent to the palace lay garages to house a number of cars, including the bishop's own limousine. I was told that the bishop could afford such a high living standard because of some farmland owned by the diocese.

I do not necessarily blame the bishop in question. He probably just inherited the set up . . .

But contrast this with Pope Francis' lifestyle when he was still Cardinal Jorge Mario Bergoglio, Archbishop of Buenos Aires, in Argentina. He chose to live in a small apartment, rather than in the elegant bishop's residence in the suburb of Olivos. He carried his own bags when traveling. He preferred public transportation to chauffeur-driven limousines. He cooked his own meals.

CHURCH LEADERSHIP AND FINANCE

When Jesus sent his apostles to preach in his name, he did not permit them to take any provisions. They were to go barefoot and without staff, as people doing penance. They should not carry money with them in any form. We can be sure that in this Jesus was prescribing what had been his own practice. In later years, when the early church was well established it became impossible to live up to Jesus' demand in all its literal rigour. St Mark's Gospel, which is based on the preaching of the apostle Peter, amended Jesus' words so as to include permission to wear sandals and use a staff (Mark 6:8–9). It was an authoritative interpretation that correctly expressed the mind of Christ.

It is clear that the injunction of the gospel still binds church leaders today. While the ordinary means of life and work are allowed (sandals and a staff), the preacher of the gospel may in no way depend on finance for his spiritual task (no gold, no silver, no copper coins). The disciple may not in any way make a profit from his service: "Give without being paid." He should be content with the hospitality offered him by the ordinary Christian. Obviously, Jesus was afraid that material riches would become an obstacle to the sowing of the word.

It is quite clear that finances are needed in the ministry and in the apostolate. The apostolic team surrounding Jesus had a common fund to pay for food and other necessities. Judas Iscariot was its treasurer. We need money to pay for church buildings, schools, hospitals, convents. But the financial organization for all this should be entrusted to capable managers. It should never overshadow the spiritual ministry.

QUESTIONS

1. What is your experience about all this? Who controls the finances in your parish and diocese? Are the bishop and the parish clergy accountable to the community for their financial dealings? Do you think they should be, or not?

2. Do you feel finances have become entangled with authority in the Church? Or do you not see any conflict? What do you consider a correct and balanced solution?

3. Do you think that your proposed solution is in harmony with what Jesus wants?

4. Is there anything you can do to consolidate or bring about that solution?

20

No institutional control without accountability

"The king summoned the managers to whom he had entrusted his money, to find out what they had gained with it." (Luke 19:14)

© Wijngaards Institute

"How on earth can I hide this from my parish council?"

DURING ONE OF MY lecture tours in Asia I was staying in college premises not far from a Church that was—and still is—a popular

Catholic pilgrimage centre. At night I could not sleep for long. Noisy parties were going on in the streets below my room till late in the morning.

At breakfast I asked Robert, the guardian of the college, my host, what the pilgrimage was all about.

"It's a long story," he said. "But I'll keep it short. As you know, we celebrate the Assumption of Our Lady in two days' time. Well, about eighty years ago an old woman, who was believed to be a saintly person, attended church on that day. And she claimed she saw a vision of Our Lady with outstretched arms hovering over her statue on the right side of the altar."

"Such claims have been made elsewhere too," I said.

"Indeed," he replied. "But other things happened. A young mother who was carrying her sick baby stepped forward and touched the statue with her baby. The child was immediately healed. Since then, every year around Assumption Day families come from far and wide to entrust their newborn babies to Mary. Mothers queue up before the statue. When they reach the front, they kneel down holding the baby and making it touch the statue. They believe it cures their baby from diseases and ensures their future health."

"It also sounds like good business for the parish," I remarked.

"Sure, it is! Our parish priest is a good businessman. People light candles all over the church. They leave gifts in front of the altar. They stuff money into the money boxes. Our parish is the richest in the diocese."

"Wonderful!," I exclaimed.

"I wish that was true," Robert said with a sigh. "It could be wonderful, but it isn't. Our parish priest uses the income to expand the business. He spends a lot of cash on redecorating the church. He has extended the parking facilities outside the building. He has now bought a plot to construct a complex of guestrooms for pilgrims . . ."

"What's wrong with that?," I asked.

"We have hundreds of poor Catholic families in the parish," Robert replied. "They have six to eight children each. Parents are periodically out of work. Then the children starve. Moreover, there is no support for their education. No money to pay for the proper dress and textbooks required in primary school. No grants to help the children enter secondary schools and, later, colleges. I joined a group of other prominent lay men and women who approached our parish priest. We pleaded for him to set up a fund to help the poor. Offering all kinds of excuses, he refused!"

"Don't you have a parish council?"

"No. We haven't. Our parish priest has rejected the idea right from the start."

ACCOUNTABILITY

You may judge the true story I narrated above somewhat extreme. Perhaps it is. But the error it manifests underlies much of the wobbly exercise of authority by ordained ministers throughout the Church. The issue at stake is accountability.

Forms of absolute rule are found in the history of peoples all over the world. Kings and chieftains imposed their will without constraint. They dominated, often brutally. They could kill and appropriate property as they wished. And we have had such dictators until this very day. At the same time the concept of the accountability of leaders began to counteract such tyranny from the earliest times known to us.

The democratic republics of Greece explicitly enforced the principle of accountability already centuries before Christ. But the same principle can be documented in the early history of the Moghuls, the Chinese, the Japanese Ainu and the Indonesian Papuans in Asia. Accountability was recognised by the Azteks and the Maya in South America. It appears among the many tribes in ancient Africa. We even find it enshrined in the culture of the Aborigines which can be dated back 50,000 years. It is very old indeed.

DID JESUS ACCEPT THE
ACCOUNTABILITY OF LEADERS?

Jesus accepted the principle of accountability for secular leaders. His parables prove the point.

Three financial managers receive varying amounts of cash from their master—one talent, two talents and five talents. The master summons them to give an account of how they have invested this wealth (Matt 25:14–30). See also: "the king summoned the managers to whom he had entrusted his money, to find out what they had gained with it" (Luke 19:11–27).

Similarly, a king requires a manager who owes him money to render an account (Matt 18:23–35).

A dishonest manager has to render an account of his dealings. He uses his last days in office to make friends of his master's creditors (Luke 16:1–13).

Also, Jesus clearly accepts accountability of disciples to the community in case of disputes. "(*As a last resort*) inform the community. And if they refuse to listen even to the community, treat them as you would a pagan or a tax collector" (Matt 18:15–17).

Did Jesus consider his disciples accountable for the spiritual power he entrusted to them? Obviously, they are accountable to God. They have to remain close to Jesus. He is the vine. They are the branches. If they stray away from him, they will be cut off like dead branches that are burnt in the fire (John 15:1–8).

But, as far as their *spiritual* authority is concerned, disciples are not accountable to outside, secular society. They can stand by their mission.

- "When you enter a home, give it your greeting. If the home is deserving, let your peace rest on it; if it is not, your peace will return to you" (Matt 10:12–13).

- "On my account you will be brought before governors and kings as witnesses to them and to the Gentiles. But when they arrest you, do not worry about what to say or how to say it. At that time it will be given to you what to say, for it will not be you speaking, but the Spirit of your Father speaking through you" (Matt 10:18–20).

PRACTICAL IMPLICATIONS

Ministers are accountable for their actions. But we need to distinguish the two kinds of authority indicated above.

All Christians have **spiritual authority** imparted through baptism and ministers more so through ordination. This includes the power to forgive sins. Is a minister accountable for what he or she does in this regard? Yes, to God in their own conscience of course, but also to higher ministerial levels to some extent. The same applies to celebrating the Eucharist, the anointing of the sick and preaching the Good News. The spiritual realm has its own rules. Higher authority can, and should, lay down some limits and regulations. But it is in no way subject to any form of democratic control. When someone goes to confession to the parish priest, the local community cannot demand to know what sin was involved or decide whether the priest should impart absolution or not.

However, to support its spiritual mission the Church has established institutions: church buildings, parish headquarters, schools, clinics, whatever. Responsibilities of persons in charge create forms of **institutional authority**. This covers administration, organization, appointment of personnel, finance, maintenance and so on. Every leader with this kind of authority, whether ordained or not, is fully accountable for all his actions.

QUESTIONS

1. What is your own experience? Do you think accountability is a good thing, or not? Is there a process of full accountability in the management of your local Church institutions? Do the faithful, through membership in diocesan and parish

councils, take part in assessing accounts of reports submitted by church leaders?

2. Do you believe things should change, or are you happy with the present arrangements?

3. How do you personally think Jesus judges the prevailing situation? Is he pleased, or disappointed?

4. Is there anything you can do to improve matters, if they need improving?

21

No small-talk sermons

"When you are brought before synagogues, rulers, and authorities, do not worry about how to defend yourselves or what to say. For at that time the Holy Spirit will teach you what to say." (Luke 12:11–12)

© Wijngaards Institute

"Nobody really knows God! Not even your bishop!"

IN THE 1990's A friend of mine invited me to visit an unusual church in Nijmegen, the Netherlands. He took me there on a

Sunday morning. Even though church attendance was beginning to decline in other parishes, this large church was packed to the roof. Most interesting: teenagers too were keen attenders.

I soon found out the reason. The parish priest, whom I shall call Rupert, preached sermons of a different kind. They were not the flimsy 'spiritual homilies' on Gospel passages delivered in other parishes. Rupert's sermons dealt with serious issues.

In fact, Rupert delivered series of high-quality instructions on key issues. For instance, one series of sermons dealt with 'God and evolution'. It presented the scientific reasons for accepting evolution. It probed the question of whether science and faith are in conflict with each other. It explained why the Genesis creation accounts do not contradict evolution, and so on.

Another series of sermons explored: "How do we know 'God' exists?" It unfolded various features of our universe requiring a 'deeper dimension'. It examined the reasons why some leading scientists refuse to accept a God. It rejected the familiar idea of the 'Supermanager God'. It pointed out that we can only speak about God in images and what this means. It invited the audience to adopt new ways of thinking and speaking about God.

Other series looked at: "How can a good 'God' allow suffering?"; "How does our Christian idea of 'God' differ from the Muslim, Hindu, Buddhist concepts of God?"; "Can we trust what TV, radio and other media say about 'God'?"; "How to understand the violent 'God' of the Old Testament?" and "What did Jesus teach about 'God'?"

When I met Rupert after Mass, he told me that he held a weekly meeting with a group of teenagers to test the contents of his next sermon.

PREACHING AT SUNDAY MASS

For evangelical Christians the sermon is the central part of a Sunday service. It usually amounts to an instruction on Bible texts that lasts for at least an hour. The preacher delivers a detailed interpretation of scriptural passages. The listeners usually have a copy of the Bible with them so that they can read the passages the preacher is speaking about. Often they also carry a notebook and pencil to record teaching they find really helpful.

In contrast to that, Catholic sermons are usually short 'homilies'. Liturgical documents present these as reflections on the readings of the day. It results in brief 'pep talks': preachers more or less repeating what was said in the readings with some explanation on how this could influence everyday life. In reality, homilies are usually entirely predictable, shallow, 'pious' talk. The situation has worsened in many countries because priests are getting older and cannot retire for lack of new vocations.

Now, of course, for Catholics the sermon is not the central part of the Eucharist. For Catholics what matters most is an immersion in the sacramental reality: the renewed self-sacrifice by Jesus and our encounter with him in holy communion. But this should not mean that the crucial instructive role of the sermon is lost.

Most teenagers and young adults find our Catholic sermons a waste of time. Worse, the pious language with its outdated imagery conflicts with our modern views of a scientific, evolving world. The sermons are one reason why many stop going to church.

WHAT DOES JESUS THINK ABOUT THIS?

Jesus preached. And he adapted the way he preached to his audience.

- To ordinary people who were only half interested in what he had to say, he presented parables. And he explains why: "This is why I speak to the crowds in parables: although they see, they don't really see; and although they hear, they don't really hear or understand." He meant that the parables would intrigue people and force them to think (read the whole of Matt 13:10–17).

- To people who were keen to listen to him, he spoke more clearly like in the sermon on the mount (Matt 5—-7).

- When talking to the Samaritan woman, he refers to ideas and images familiar to her: living water, worship on the mountain, the coming of the messiah (John 4:4–26).

- Addressing the priests in the temple, on the day they carried water from the pool of Siloam to the temple compound, Jesus again uses images they understood (John 7:37–39).

- When arguing with the scribes and pharisees, he employs the legal terms they were used to (Matt 13:13–36).

Jesus obviously expected his Apostles to do the same when preaching. Preaching was their main task. They were to boldly enter every village and every town. They could do so with authority. They were commissioned to preach. "If anyone will not welcome you or listen to your words, leave that home or town and shake the dust off your feet. Truly I tell you, it will be more bearable for Sodom and Gomorrah on the day of judgment than for that town" (Matt 10:14–15).

And, predicting the persecution they would face in the future, he reassures them that they will be able to explain the message to each different audience in an appropriate way. "When you are brought before synagogues, rulers and authorities, do not worry about how to defend yourselves or what to say. For at that time the Holy Spirit will teach you what to say" (Luke 12:11–12).

The Acts of the Apostles show how the Apostle Paul adapted his approach to different audiences. A clear example is his speech on the philosophers' hill, the Areopagus in Athens. "People of Athens! I see that in every way you are very religious. For as I walked around and looked carefully at your objects of worship, I even found an altar with this inscription: 'to an unknown god'. So you are ignorant of the very thing you worship—and this is what I am going to proclaim to you. The God who made the world and everything in it is the Lord of heaven and earth and does not live in temples built by human hands . . ." (Acts 17:22–24; read more fully here: Acts 17:1–34).

QUESTIONS

1. What is your experience of the Sunday homilies? Positive, negative? Do sermons convincingly proclaim Jesus' message to people of our day and age?

2. Do sermons benefit our teenagers and educated adults who are facing serious assaults by the religion-ignorant, or often religion-hostile, media of our secular age?

3. If Jesus lived in our contemporary age, what would his sermons be like?

4. If matters need improving in your part of the world, what can you do about it?

22

Authority reform—ministry in times to come

"Jesus said:'Have you never read what David did when he and his companions were hungry and in need? During the high priesthood of Abiathar, he entered the house of God and ate the consecrated bread, which was lawful only for priests. And he gave some to his companions as well." (Mark 2:25–26; see 1 Samuel 21:1–6; 22:20–23)

"I must have dropped my wedding ring while walking through the maze. Can your drone retrieve it?"

YEARS AGO, AT A recollection day for youngsters, I was asked how many languages Jesus spoke. "Aramaic was his own language," I said, "and he probably managed a smattering of Greek, as most Jews did in his time. But he would definitely not have understood English."

Judy, a tall girl with long hair which framed her penetrating dark blue eyes, was visibly upset by this. "Jesus was God," she protested. "He was omniscient. He knew everything. He must have known English. In fact, it would probably have taken him no more than five minutes to fill in *The Times* crossword puzzle. It was all there in his mind!"

"Hold on," I said. "Yes, Jesus' humanity conveyed/carried/communicated divinity. But that did not affect his being a hundred percent human. Did Jesus not need to use his feet to walk from one place to the next? Wasn't he tired and hungry at the end of a day, like anyone else? Did he not need a rest from time to time?"

"Yes," she admitted reluctantly. "But that's different, just physical. Omniscience resides in the mind!"

"I'm afraid you are wrong," I replied. "Human limitations affected Jesus's mind. Like his contemporaries, Jesus could not imagine what an electric train was going to be like, or a motor car, an aeroplane, a TV set, a computer. As a human being he was in all respects like everyone else—just as he wanted to be. He called himself the 'Son of Man', an Aramaic expression for 'the ordinary person'. He even could make mistakes, like remembering things wrongly."

"Make mistakes?!," she exclaimed. "Surely not! Can you prove that?"

"Yes," I said. "Jesus got it wrong when he said that Abiathar was high priest when David ate of the consecrated loaves. We read in the first Book of Samuel that the high priest at the time was Abimelech and that Abiathar became high priest afterwards. Since Jesus had no personal copy of the Bible to consult, he had to remember texts by heart—from what he had heard at Sabbath readings. Confusing the names of Abimelech and Abiathar is the kind of memory slip anyone of us could have made. And it did not invalidate the point that Jesus was making. It simply was a human thing to do."

AMPLIFYING JESUS' TEACHING
IN TIMES TO COME

John's Gospel differs from those of Mark, Matthew and Luke in that it explicitates/unfolds Jesus' intentions. It addresses especially Hellenistic [= Greek speaking] audiences at the end of the first century. It translates Jesus' original Aramaic sayings into the more sophisticated language and thinking of the Graeco-Roman world.[1]

John's account of the Last Supper is also unique. It offers a long speech by Jesus in which he prepares the disciples for the years to come. The gist of it is that he himself will no longer be among them in his physical appearance. But he will remain present in a spiritual way, through his Spirit. The Spirit will make clear how Jesus' intentions should be interpreted in fresh unexpected challenges of future times to come. "I have much more to tell you, but now it is too hard for you to understand. But when the Spirit of truth comes, he will lead you into all the truth. He will not speak on his own, but he will tell you what he hears and will speak of things to come" (John 16: 12–13).

These are crucial words indeed. And how will the Spirit speak? Will the Spirit reveal Jesus' mind only through ordained church leaders, through priests, bishops, popes? The answer is: No! The Spirit will operate throughout the community.

"There are different kinds of gifts, but the same Spirit distributes them. There are different kinds of service, but the same Lord. There are different kinds of working, but in all of them and in everyone it is the same God at work. Now to each one the manifestation of the Spirit is given for the common good. To one there is given through the Spirit a message of wisdom, to another a message of knowledge by means of the same Spirit, to another faith by the same Spirit, to another gifts of healing by that one Spirit, to

1. Wijngaards, *Gospel of John*, 11–32.

another miraculous powers, to another prophecy, to another distinguishing between spirits, to another speaking in different kinds of tongues, and to still another the interpretation of tongues. All these are the work of one and the same Spirit, and God distributes them to each one, just as he determines" (1 Cor 12:28).

QUESTIONS

1. What is your experience about the challenges of our modern age? Our science-driven technological world creates fresh possibilities which also pose new moral dilemmas. Do you feel spiritual authorities respond adequately to such challenges?

2. In our new secular social climate, do Church leaders also listen to the Spirit speaking through professionals—biologists, psychologists, sociologists you name it? Are you happy with the situation, or not?

3. Do you think Jesus would have listened to the advice of secular experts?

4. If a change is required, what you can do to bring it about?

23

Authority reform— women deacons

"The Twelve were with him, and also some women who had been cured of evil spirits and diseases: Mary (called Magdalene) from whom seven demons had come out; Joanna the wife of Chuza, the manager of Herod's household; Susanna; and many others. These women were helping to support them out of their own means." (Luke 8:1–4)

"Please, leave her! At least here she's far from my pulpit!"

IN THE 1980's, AS Vicar General of the Mill Hill Missionaries, I visited one of our members. He had served in Kenya for a while. On his return he had been entrusted with a rural parish in the North of England.

After lunch he told me that he had to conduct a meeting for Auxiliaries in that region. One way of collecting funds for the missions was for Catholic families to keep a 'mission box' in their home in which they themselves or friends could deposit coins when occasions arose. Auxiliaries, mainly women, volunteered to collect these mission boxes every so many months. They would open them, count the contents, send the proceeds to a central account and return the mission boxes to their various homes.

"I try to make these meetings worthwhile," Father told me. "Would you be prepared to come along and give them a little pep talk?"

I said I would.

When my turn came at the meeting, I talked to the group about the need for the Church to re-instate the diaconate for women. I narrated how ordained women deacons had ministered in East and West during the first millennium and how their service was, regretfully, discontinued mainly because of fear that women in their periods might contaminate the sacred space surrounding the altar.

The response of the women stunned me. Though some were pleasantly surprised and supportive, a large group voiced fierce opposition. "You're contradicting the Pope!," one shouted at me. "He's infallible. You are not!"

When I discussed this with the priest later, back in his house, he sighed. "You have no clue of how traditional some priests are in this area," he said. "Recently, at a deanery meeting, when the idea of a woman reading Scripture or even preaching was raised, one parish priest declared: 'I will never tolerate a womb, imagine a *womb?*, on my pulpit!' . . ."

Do I need to say more?

WOMEN DEACONS

The first seven deacons ordained by the Apostles were all men. But soon also women became deacons. Paul says: "I commend to you our sister Phoebe, a deacon [= *diakonos*] of the church in Cenchreae. I ask you to receive her in the Lord in a way worthy of his people and to give her any help she may need from you, for she has looked after many people, including myself" (Rom 16:1–2).

1 Tim 3:8–13 mentions both male and female deacons. "Deacons *(male)* must be reliable etc. . . . (vs. 8–10). In the same way, the women *(female deacons)* are to be worthy of respect, not malicious talkers but temperate and trustworthy in everything (vs. 11). A deacon *(male)* must be faithful to his wife and must manage his children and his household well (vs. 12). Those who have served as deacons [*diakonisantes* = both *male* and *female*] with distinction will achieve a high status and great assurance in their faith in Christ Jesus" (vs. 13).

We have abundant evidence about female deacons from Church Fathers, historical records and tombstones. We have texts of the ordination rite for women deacons from the third century AD. They show that the rite was substantially identical to that of male deacons and fully sacramental.[1]

What would Jesus have said about this development?

FORESHADOWED IN THE GOSPELS

Jesus did not explicitly deal with the diaconate. It was the Apostles who established it as a separate sacramental ministry (Acts 6:1–6). We can be sure they knew this was the kind of thing Jesus would have wanted, for women as well as for men.

We find also women among the disciples who travelled with Jesus. "The Twelve were with him, and also some women who had been cured of evil spirits and diseases: Mary (called Magdalene) from whom seven demons had come out; Joanna the wife of Chuza, the manager of Herod's household; Susanna; and many

1. Wijngaards, *Women Deacons in the Early Church*, 145–88.

others. These women were helping to support them out of their own means" (Luke 8:1–4). Notice that these were practical women.

- Mary of Magdala stood under the cross when Jesus was crucified giving support to Jesus' mother (John 19:25–26). She made sure to note where Jesus was buried (Mark 15:47). On Easter morning she went to Jesus' tomb to anoint his body and became one of the first witnesses of the resurrection (John 20:1–18).

- Joanna came from a family of managers. Her husband oversaw the domestic arrangements in the palace of Herod Antipas. She accompanied Mary of Magdala to help her anoint Jesus' body.

Then we have the story of Mary and Martha. Martha is obviously running the show. She invites Jesus into their home. She provides food, drink and other facilities to Jesus and his apostles. She was obviously keen to listen to Jesus' teaching, but when her sister Mary, sitting at Jesus' feet, leaves the hospitality service to her alone, she objects. Jesus gives her a gentle rebuke: "Martha, Martha, you are worried and distracted by many things; but only one thing is necessary. Mary has chosen the better part, which shall not be taken away from her" (Luke 10:38–42).

Another story of Mary and Martha occurs in John's Gospel (John 11:1–44). They are sisters of Jesus' friend Lazarus. Probably they are the same persons mentioned earlier by Luke. When Lazarus dies, Jesus goes out of his way to visit them. Again it is Martha who takes the lead. While Mary stays in the house, Martha runs out to meet Jesus. Responding to Jesus she expresses her faith three times:

- "If you had been here, my brother would not have died" (vs. 21).

- "I know my brother will rise again in the resurrection at the last day" (vs 24).

- And to Jesus' words 'I am resurrection and life', she replies: "I believe that you are the Messiah, the Son of God, who is to come into the world" (vs. 27).

After having called her sister Mary, Martha then leads Jesus to the tomb in which Lazarus had been buried four days earlier. The stone in front of the tomb was removed. Jesus calls Lazarus out. And he comes out, still wrapped in funeral linen—but again fully alive.

It is obvious that Jesus accepted such competent women who both provided valuable service (*diakonia*) and who possessed exemplary faith.

QUESTIONS

1. What is your experience about women's ministry in the Church? Did you find women can provide leadership, a caring service and their own charisms to the ministry? Or have you been disappointed? Do you agree with church authorities who are reluctant to reinstall the age-old diaconate of women?

2. Do you personally think Jesus would exclude women from the ordained diaconate in our time?

3. Is there anything you can do in this matter?

24

Authority Reform— talk to opponents

"You have heard that it was said, 'Love your neighbour and hate your enemy.' But I tell you, love your enemies and pray for those who persecute you, that you may be children of your Father in heaven." (Matt 5:43–45)

"Simple enough! I'll have him for dinner!"

CHRIST'S IDEA OF AUTHORITY IN THE CHURCH

THIS STORY RECOUNTS MY clash with a Polish bishop and a surprising outcome. Let me paint the setting.

In the 1980's and 1990's, while teaching in the *Missionary Institute London* and going for lecture trips to India, I also ran a Centre for Adult Faith Formation called 'Housetop'. The Archbishop of Westminster had asked me to provide spiritual support to individuals caught up in the so-called 'Sects & Cults'. This was because of my experience in the Far East from which those cults originated.

Well, the Council of European Bishops Conferences convoked a consultation on *'Sects and Fringe Religious Groups in Europe'* in March 1998. The event took place in Vienna. I had been asked to be part of the delegation flown in from England. There were 120 participants. On the 7th of March I presented to the assembly a paper entitled *'God and our new Selves. Why there is the need of a new Catechesis'.*[1]

In my paper I set out the background of the attraction of cults and fringe groups to teenagers. I pointed out that sociology showed an enormous transformation affecting educated Europeans. God was disappearing from everyday life. Societies has become mixed, pluriform and fragmented. People's personal autonomy was taking over from traditional morality. And most of all, from having been 'security-seekers' depending on others, people were growing into 'fulfilment-seekers': persons intent to realise their own potential to the full. I pleaded for the Church to take the new Europeans seriously and treat them in a supportive pastoral way.

The reaction to my paper was explosive. Some participants agreed, but many were scandalised by it. In particular one young Polish bishop whose name I have forgotten, was furious. He shouted at me that I was surrendering Catholic doctrine and morality to the corroding current pagan mentality of modern times. The chairman of the session stopped the debate . . .

Then the big surprise. Late in the afternoon, after all the business sessions, we ended the day by celebrating Mass. I had been randomly chosen to be one of the two concelebrants on that day. I

1. Wijngaards, "God and Our New Selves," 172–93.

106

went to the sacristy, put on the vestments and waited for the main celebrant to show up. Well, lo and behold, it turned out to be the same Polish bishop! He too was a little taken aback seeing me, but then got on with the job. I stood at his side at the altar. When the 'peace-giving' ritual came along, we looked each other in the face and did just that: gave peace.

Afterwards at supper we sat together. Like myself he too had studied in Rome. We could communicate in Italian . . . We chatted about all kind of things. Somehow it broke the ice. We did not agree on our assessment of the situation in the Church, but we belonged to the same family . . .

DIVISIONS IN THE CHURCH

Two wings dominate our present Church community. Conservatives on the right fiercely defend what they see as established Church tradition. They have been strongly bolstered by Popes John Paul II and Benedict XIV in previous decades. Progressives on the left demand reforms, based on new theological insights and pastoral needs.

The alarming thing is that the two wings rarely communicate with each other. They talk to themselves. Both the left and the right wing have their own circles of communication: associations, websites, and social media. Both wings have even conquered intellectual control of a number of universities, colleges and seminaries.

Of course, the two wings clash online. But there is no real sitting down together to listen to the other person's concerns and to explain one's own reasons for thinking differently. Trustful person-to-person contact is rare.

JESUS' THINKING ABOUT REAL DIALOGUE

Jesus revealed precious new truths about God. Truth is important and should not be tampered with. Jesus' teaching should be defended at all costs. We may not tolerate it being diminished or dented by anyone . . .

That may be so. But how should we treat a person who we think is not faithful to Jesus' teaching? Strike him or her down? How would Jesus treat such an opponent?

It is useful here to turn to some remarkable passages in the Sermon on the Mount. What about **criminals**? Amazingly, Jesus tells us not to retaliate with force. "I tell you, do not resist an evil person. If anyone slaps you on the right cheek, turn to them the other cheek also. And if anyone wants to sue you and take your shirt, hand over your coat as well. If anyone forces you to go one mile (to carry a burden), go with them another mile" (Matt 5:38– 42). Although we may need police to protect our safety, we should still treat a criminal as a friend.

And what about people who oppose us directly, who want to harm us, our **enemies**? Here too Jesus' attitude is revolutionary. "You have heard that it was said, 'Love your neighbour and hate your enemy'. But I tell you, love your enemies and pray for those who persecute you, that you may be children of your Father in heaven. He causes his sun to rise on the evil and the good, and sends rain on the righteous and the unrighteous. If you love those who love you, what reward will you get? Are not even the tax collectors doing that? And if you greet only your own people, what are you doing more than others? Do not even pagans do that?" (Matt 5:43–47). In other words: we should treat our opponents with kindness and understanding.

Jesus must have been appalled by Church practices in previous centuries: persecution and torture by the Inquisition; the burning at the stake of 'heretics'.

QUESTIONS

1. What is your own experience about communication between progressives and conservatives? Do they communicate at all? Or do they just condemn each other from a distance? Have

you witnessed Church leaders provide pastoral support even
to persons whom they believe to hold erroneous ideas?

2. What would Jesus have done about it?

3. Is there anything you can do to bring members of the two
   opposing wings together in a friendly and fruitful exchange
   of views?

25

Authority Reform—step by step

"The kingdom of heaven is like yeast that a woman took and mixed into about sixty pounds of flour until it worked all through the dough." (Matt 13:34)

"Why couldn't he go down one branch at a time?!"

THE CHANGE OF RELIGIOUS dress for Sisters in India has been a drawn out, and at times turbulent, story. In the early 1980's I was invited to give some lectures at a renewal seminar of a large Indian religious congregation. The meeting took place at the *Mater Dei Institute* in Old Goa. The participants were mainly local superiors of schools and convents.

I noticed that most Sisters were wearing light brown saris, but some were still dressed in traditional white habits. I asked one of the Sisters, whom I shall call 'Theresamma' about this.

"Well," she told me. "It's a long story. As our dress we had inherited a medieval habit from Europe. After Vatican II both practical reasons and cultural adaptation demanded a change, but there was much opposition. Many sisters themselves and their families considered the loss of the habit a reduction of status. Fortunately, we had a wise Superior General who brought about reform in stages."

"What stages?," I asked.

"You won't believe this," she said. "The first stage was the abolition of the 'chastity corset'. This was a short dress, from the waist down, that sisters were supposed to wear while having a bath or taking a shower. It was meant to save them from seeing their own naked underbody . . . Of course, it was ridiculous and unhygienic. It was dropped without too much opposition."

"My goodness!," I said.

"The second stage was to get rid of the headpiece, the so-called 'coif'. This was an elaborate structure. It consisted of a white cotton cap secured by a strip across the forehead and a white 'wimple' to cover the neck and cheeks. Over all this hung a short cape of starched linen, known as a 'guimpe', which covered the top of the chest. The whole thing required that practically all hair was removed from the scalp. The coif was an abomination in the hot climate of India. I remember the relief when it was replaced by a simple veil. It also meant we could grow long hair again."

"How liberating!," I exclaimed.

"Indeed," Theresamma replied. "And not too much opposition here either. That came with stage three. As you know, the traditional religious habit was a 'tunic' worn underneath, with a 'scapular' on top of it, a kind of apron draped from the front and back. The whole was kept together by a belt, the so-called 'cincture'. When, at one of our chapters, the Superior General wanted for cultural reasons to replace this with an Indian-style sari, many Sisters objected. Others applauded the move. The General showed her wisdom again by suggesting that adopting the sari would not be opposed as an obligation. Each Sister could and can choose for herself."

"Did it not lead to confusion?," I asked.

"No, it didn't. And, although it was a slow process, the sari is winning the contest. The number of Sisters still wearing the old habit is dwindling rapidly!"

WORKING FOR REFORM

Many progressive thinkers in the Catholic Church are dreaming of massive changes. And for them, the sooner they happen the better. They believe that, after centuries of mismanagement in the Church, the way forward lies in boldly implementing a drastic programme of colossal reforms. One campaigner quoted Johann von Goethe at me, the nineteenth-century German statesman: "Boldness has genius, power and magic in it. Act now!"

Such campaigners overlook many key factors. It will take a considerable time to disentangle church structures that have been used for centuries. They usually involve many elements: buildings, finances, established customs, specific jobs and tasks. But most of all they overlook the human factor.

People need time to adjust to a new reality. They have to fully grasp the reasons for change. They have to experience the advantages of the new system. Reform that is introduced too radically and too fast will totally alienate traditionalists and confuse the ordinary faithful in the middle.

What did Jesus think about all this?

JESUS RECOMMENDS A
GRADUAL APPROACH

Through some of his parables Jesus taught that the Christian faith would grow in steps. "The kingdom of heaven is like a mustard seed, which a man took and planted in his field. Though it is the smallest of all seeds, yet when it grows, it is the largest of garden plants and becomes a tree, so that the birds come and perch in its branches" (Matt 13:31–32).

Even more telling is this: "The kingdom of heaven is like yeast that a woman took and mixed into about sixty pounds of flour until it worked all through the dough" (Matt 13:34). Jesus refers here to a huge jar, as they have been found by archaeology, a jar that could contain 25 kilograms of flour. Just a small handful of yeast would slowly but surely leaven all the dough in one or two days' time.

Jesus' step-by-step approach is also well demonstrated in the way he gradually prepared Peter for his role as head of the apostolic twelve.

Jesus called Peter from his job as a fisherman (Mark 1:16–20). It was his home in Capernaum that Jesus visited when he cured Peter's mother-in-law (Matt 8:14). And it was Peter's boat that Jesus used when he instructed the crowd (Luke 5:3). Peter asked Jesus for clarification of a parable (Matt 15:15).

However, Peter could be unpredictable. One moment he displayed remarkable insight when proclaiming that Jesus was truly the Son of God (Matt 16:15–18). Then, failing to understand what was really at stake, he rebuked his Master when Jesus prophesied his suffering and death (Mark 8:32–33). And he requested Jesus for a special place in heaven as a reward for his faithful service (Matt 19:27–28).

When Jesus was being interrogated in the high priest's house, Peter let Jesus down, denying three times that he was one of Jesus' disciples (Mark 14:66–72). He regretted it bitterly. Jesus responded, not by discarding Peter but by allowing him to be the first Apostle to see him after the resurrection (Luke 22:31–32). And, in a final encounter at the lake of Galilee, he accepted Peter's renewed commitment and entrusted him again with pastoral leadership over the disciples (John 21:15–17).

QUESTIONS

1. What is your experience regarding implementing reforms? Did you find a slow process provides a result? Or a rigorous sudden imposition of changes? Do you agree that any adaptations in prevailing Church 'doctrines' and practices need to be accompanied by explanations, by a series of instructions that address both traditionalists and the body of the faithful? What is your position in all this?

2. What do you think Jesus' approach would have been in our day and age?

3. Does this require any immediate action on your part?

26

Authority Reform—allow more regional variation

"Jesus stood and said in a loud voice, 'Let anyone who is thirsty come to me and drink. Whoever believes in me, as Scripture has said, rivers of living water will flow from within them." (John 7:37)

© Wijngaards Institute

"I suddenly grasp: if the Church is a 'Mother Church', she can give birth to a variety of infant churches!"

FROM 1964 I TAUGHT in St John's Major Seminary, Hyderabad, India, for almost two decades. During that time I got to know many parishes there. This story is about a parish that lay on the outskirts of the city.

You must remember that during that period many reforms initiated by the Second Vatican Council were being implemented. They affected the liturgy in many ways. Not only could the Eucharist now be celebrated in one of the local languages. Many cultural customs were being introduced.

The parish priest of the parish in question, whom I will call Chinnappa Reddy, looked after the main Italian-style church in the built up areas of the town. But he also had to care for outstations in villages lying outside the city boundaries.

Fr Chinnappa told me that there was a world of difference in the way the Eucharist was celebrated in the centre and outside town.

"People in our main church come from many different backgrounds," he said. "They are also used to the way Mass has been celebrated in the past. They come in and genuflect as they used to do before. I say Mass in English. Our choir presents English hymns, but occasionally they revert to the old well-known Latin songs. I distribute holy communion on the hand but also on the tongue."

"In the outside villages it's a totally different story. At Mass everyone sits on the floor round a low altar, Indian style. The prayers are in Telugu. We use Indian gestures. We don't genuflect, we bow."

Knowing that I myself was used to celebrate Indian style Masses, he invited me to preside at a local village on a Sunday. I did.

It was a wonderful experience. It took place in a school hall. I sat cross-legged on the floor behind a low altar. The whole congregation surrounded me, all sitting on the floor. At the beginning of Mass a local teacher lit the Indian oil lamp, the *deepam*, in front of the altar. The readings and prayers were all in Telugu. At the offertory, children brought up bread and wine, as well as flowers with which I could decorate the altar. Incense was used to honour the sacred gifts while I performed the *arati*, the rite by which the gifts are lifted up and moved round in a circle. During the words of consecration, people got up on both knees and made a deep bow. At communion, people would take a host and dip it into the consecrated wine before consuming it.

"Some persons criticise me for maintaining the old order in our main church," Fr Chinnappa said to me. "I think they are wrong. Each section of the community deserves to be treated the way that corresponds to their needs. Uniformity would be a mistake."

REGIONAL VARIATIONS

In recent centuries there has been a trend in the Catholic Church to be obsessed by 'uniformity'. Of course, we are One Holy Catholic Church. And yes, the same basic doctrines of faith apply everywhere. But there is no reason why, as far as customs and practices are concerned, there should not be more regional variation between countries and continents.

In fact, there are already such differences.

The Lebanon's Catholic Maronite Rite allows married men to be ordained priests. And there are striking variations in the way the Eucharist is celebrated in the Catholic Syriac Rite of the Syro-Malabar community in India and the Catholic Alexandrian Rite in Egypt and Ethiopia.

Moreover, the Second Vatican Council introduced the use of the vernacular in each country or part of a country, with other cultural adaptations.

WHAT DID JESUS THINK ABOUT IT?

Jesus public ministry lasted only for three years. Moreover, no established church communities had yet been set up. So, we cannot make a parallel with the specific needs of later times, especially when the Christian faith took root worldwide. Still, we can learn from Jesus' attitude and way of acting.

Galilee and Judea, both provinces of Palestine, contrasted markedly in Jesus' time. Galilee was rural, Judea heavily urbanised. Jesus was well aware of it. He adapted his approach to do justice to the needs of each.

Galilee in fact was looked down upon by many Palestinians. "Can anything good come from Nazareth?!," Nathanael exclaims (John 1:46). Galileans downrated themselves. When Jesus proclaimed his mission in the synagogue of Nazareth, the other villagers reject him. "Is he not the carpenter's son? Is his mother not called Mary? And are not his brothers [= relatives] James and Joseph and Simon and Judas? And are not all his sisters with us? Where then did this man get all these things?" (Matt 13:15–58). Because most Galileans lived from farming, fishing and tending flocks of sheep, it is in Galilee that Jesus presents parables based on those crafts.

On the other hand, Judea enjoyed a more sophisticated, urbanised life style. The temple at Jerusalem dominated the region, not just religiously, but also economically. Income from tourists and pilgrims brought wealth to the region. Jesus recognised those traits and consciously adapted his approach accordingly. The infancy story of Jesus as a boy questioning the priests in the temple (Luke 2:41–52) foreshadows that.

The Jews celebrated the Feast of Tabernacles to give thanks for their crops, but also God's promise that he would *tabernacle* (dwell) among them. During that feast Jesus appeared in the temple (John 7:1–52). In the crowded temple courts, he proclaimed in effect that the Father was *tabernacling* (*living*) in himself. And on the final day, when water was carried into the temple from the pool of Siloam, "Jesus stood and said in a loud voice, 'Let anyone who is thirsty come to me and drink. Whoever believes in me, as Scripture has said, rivers of living water will flow from within them.' By this he meant the Spirit, whom those who believed in him were later to receive. Up to that time the Spirit had not been given, since Jesus had not yet been glorified" (John 7:37–38).

Again, Jerusalem was used to festive processions with palms into the temple area. Originally the ark of the covenant, on top of which *Yahweh's* invisible presence was believed to reside, would be carried into the temple, re-enacting its first entry under King David. In Jesus' time one annual event commemorated the liberation of Jerusalem under the Maccabees in 141 BC (1 Macc 13:51–62). Jesus deliberately imitates this custom when entering Jerusalem sitting on a donkey and surrounded by people wearing palms. People chanted: "Hosanna to the Son of David. Blessed is he who comes in the name of the Lord" (Mark 11:1–11).

QUESTIONS

Have you any personal experience of the enormous cultural and social differences between various Catholic communities, reflecting the countries and continents they come from?

Do you believe that when reforms in church practice are agreed upon, the implementation of these reforms should be imposed everywhere at the same time? Or should the bishops' conferences in those countries and continents be allowed to introduce changes *gradually,* according to local needs and requirements?

Do you personally think Jesus would have recommended regional variations in our massive international Catholic community? Or would he have preferred immediate world-wide uniformity?

Is there anything you can do regarding this complex question?

27

Authority Reform—can a schism be avoided?

"On hearing Jesus' words, many of his disciples said, 'This is a hard teaching. Who can accept it?'... From this time many of his disciples turned back and no longer followed him." (John 6:60.66)

© Wijngaards Institute

"You must also serve meat, Father. Otherwise, I'll join the Baptists!"

IN THE 1980's, WHILE I was still Vicar General of the Mill Hill Missionaries, I had been on visitation in France. By car I had visited some of our retired missionaries who, after return from overseas missions, helped out in French parishes. Then I was on my way from French Lyons across the Alps to Geneva in Switzerland for a meeting at the World Council of Churches.

Just outside Lyons I saw a priest, wearing a black cassock and white collar, standing on the roadside asking for a lift. I stopped the car. When he was seated, we introduced ourselves to each other. I will call him Father Paschal.

When I asked him about his ministry, he told me: "I'm still a parish priest, but I am a follower of Bishop Lefebvre."

"Bishop Lefebvre?!," I exclaimed. "But Lefebvre is no longer in full communion with the Church!" Bishop Marcel Lefebvre led a conservative bloc during the sessions of Council Vatican II. He did not accept many decisions by the Council. He cut himself from the Church in 1988 by consecrating four bishops against strict prohibitions from the Vatican.

"Well, I agree with Bishop Lefebvre," he replied. "The Second Vatican Council has made many mistakes. It tolerates 'religious liberty', ecumenism, collegiality and other nonsense."

"They are not nonsense," I reacted. "They are requirements in our modern age and in harmony with our Catholic faith."

"Well, you're misguided," Father Paschal declared. "I am sure you say Mass in the vernacular?"

"Yes, I do."

"Well, that's another atrocity introduced by Vatican II. Latin is our sacred language. It should not be abandoned. I always celebrate the Eucharist in Latin."

Our discussion came to nothing. When we arrived in Geneva, he took leave from me saying that he would travel on to Écône, where the headquarters of Lefebvre's Pius X Society was located.

SCHISM AMONG JESUS' FOLLOWERS

Hundreds of larger and smaller schisms have happened in the history of the Church. The majority were due to traditionalists not willing to accept a new understanding of doctrine or practice.

It already started in Jesus' time. Chapter Six in St John's Gospel narrates how Jesus on the shores of lake Galilee performed the miracle of the multiplication of the bread and the fish. Five thousand of his followers benefitted from this (John 6:10). When Jesus crossed over to the other side of the lake, a large number of them followed him there keen to hear more of his teaching.

In the synagogue of Capernaum Jesus announced that, like the manna the Jews ate in the desert, he was the Bread of Life. He repeatedly said: "You will eat my flesh and drink my blood," referring to the establishment of the Eucharist (John 6:25–59).

This was a new development a group of followers did not want to accept. It went against everything they believed as Jews. "On hearing it, many of his disciples said, 'This is a hard teaching. Who can accept it?'" (John 6:60) In spite of Jesus' pleading, they turned their backs to him. "From this time many of his disciples turned back and no longer followed him" (John 6:66).

In response. Jesus did not change his teaching. "Jesus asked the Twelve: 'Do you want to leave me too?' Simon Peter answered him, 'Lord, to whom shall we go? You have the words of eternal life.'" (John 6:67–68)

NOT WILLING TO ACCEPT A
NEW UNDERSTANDING

At the Last Supper Jesus foretold that future generations of his disciples would need to re-absorb and reformulate his teaching within their own world. And he promised that his Spirit, active in them, would be able to perform this task. "All this I have spoken while still with you. But the Advocate, the Holy Spirit, whom the Father will send in my name, will teach you all things and will remind you of everything I have said to you" (John 14:26–27).

Again: "I have much more to say to you, more than you can now bear. But when he, the Spirit of truth, comes, he will guide you into all the truth. He will not speak on his own; he will speak only what he hears, and he will tell you what is yet to come" (John 16:12–13).

Jesus also foresaw the possibility of schisms. In his prayer at the Last Supper, he prayed for unity among the disciples. "My prayer is not for them (the Twelve) alone. I pray also for those who will believe in me through their message, that all of them may be one, Father, just as you are in me and I am in you. May they also be in us so that the world may believe that you have sent me. I have given them the glory that you gave me, that they may be one as we are one — I in them and you in me — so that they may be brought to complete unity" (John 17:20–23).

But Jesus' prayer for unity does not imply that this unity should be maintained at the cost of rejecting the new developments championed by his Spirit (John 14:26–27; 16:12–13).

QUESTIONS

1. What about yourself? Are you conservative, progressive or middle of the road?

2. Have you had any experience with traditionalist groupings in the Church? Did you find that they form closed circles in which members continuously push each other to resist change? Do you think their worries and concerns are taken seriously enough by others in the Church?

3. Where do you think Jesus stands: more on the traditionalist or on the progressive side?

4. Is there anything you can do to avoid schisms to happen? Can you, somehow, break into closed circles and initiate a meaningful discussion? Vatican II reforms were often not accepted by people because the justification for them had not been properly explained. Can you supplement the information needed?

28

Authority Reform— it will happen!

"After six days Jesus took with him Peter, James and John the brother of James, and led them up a high mountain by themselves. There he was transfigured before them." (Matt 17:1–2)

"Come right in, Father! You are top scorer of the month!"

IN THE 1980's I used to spend some months every year as a touring lecturer in India. On one occasion a bishop in the tribal area of

Jharkhand State invited me to give a biblical seminar to his priests in the diocese. I will call him Bishop Bartholomew. I was given accommodation in Bishop's House.

One evening, after supper, the bishop invited me to his private study. Over a cup of hot chocolate he told me an interesting story.

"I was consecrated a bishop just after Vatican II," he said. "And, to tell you the truth, I was upset by many of the changes introduced by the Council. A new local liturgy? But we had spent decades to teach people the international western rite! Being friendly to Hindus? But they were our feared opponents! More freedom for religious Sisters? But how then could we keep them under control?!"

"So, what happened?," I asked. "You accept Vatican II now, don't you?"

"Yes, I do. Well, this is my story . . . It began when I was consulting a number of my staff. The old Bishop's House was too small. Priests who visited me had nowhere to stay. And whenever I called together all the priests in the diocese for a meeting, I had to rent the hall in a local school . . . Some of my staff members advised me to build a new wing with a hall on the ground floor and guest-rooms on top. One was more radical. 'Tear down this old house', he advised me, 'and build a bigger one.'"

"It must have been a difficult time for you," I said.

"Indeed, it was. But then a conversion happened. I was sitting in my small local chapel reflecting on the predicament and praying . . . I recognised the old Bishop's House was a shambles. It had started as a small western-style house. Then, at various stages, new parts were added: a new living room with up-to-date bathroom facilities; then a shack to house a better-style kitchen; then a floor on top of the house to create more bedrooms; then a wider verandah on which the bishop could sit in the evenings and talk to people . . . And while I was thinking about all this, another thought suddenly struck me. My house was a heap of accretions but so was the Church! Jesus' teaching had accumulated all kinds of imported additions over the centuries: Greek and Roman customs, beliefs and practices from the European Middle Ages and-so-on. It struck me that the Church too needed a thorough overhaul just like Bishop's House . . ."

"Well, that's marvellous!," I said.

"Indeed. It shook me. Next day I want over to a nearby college where a good friend of mine was teaching. He was a Belgian Jesuit. I told him about my new insight—he smiled and congratulated me. Then he gave me more background information about some of Vatican II's reforms. We had more such discussions afterwards. I tore down the old Bishop's House and built the new one. I also became a firm supporter of the new changes."

I admired Bishop Bartholomew for his honesty and intelligence.

IMPLEMENTING CHURCH REFORMS

Church reform can take time and require major efforts on the part of leaders in the Church. The Council that initiated enormous changes, before Vatican II, was the Council of Trent. It met for 24 sessions between 1545 and 1563, and spanned the reign of three popes. It was the Catholic Church's response to the Protestant Reformation which had caused large sections of the faithful to split off from the Mother Church.

And, by golly, did the Church of that time need reforms! Corruption was rampant in the Curia. In most countries sons of aristocratic rulers were appointed bishops, disregarding their spiritual qualities, to be allies in politics. Priests were ordained without proper education. Indulgences were sold for money. Immorality was tolerated in many convents. Trent prescribed countermeasures which have benefitted the Church ever since.

But implementing Trent's reforms took a lot of hard work. In many parts of the Church decades passed before the new discipline was in place. Credit goes to the thousands of bishops, priests, religious superiors and others who gradually, with a lot of patience, hardship and diplomatic skill, fought for the reforms to be realised. Being a reformer is not an easy task.

WHAT WOULD JESUS THINK ABOUT IT ALL?

Jesus, of course, has been the most prominent and successful religious reformer in humankind's history. His revelation that God is Love and his teaching that loving the neighbour is our highest duty have, over the centuries, constructively impacted the way we humans relate to each other. Christians are the largest religious community on our planet. But Jesus also foresaw the enormous challenges to come—for himself and his followers.

In this context, Jesus' transfiguration on Mount Tabor is very significant. Jesus was on his way to Jerusalem. It would cause him incredible pain and suffering. It would also result in his triumphant resurrection. A vision overwhelmed Jesus. "His face shone like the sun, and his clothes became as white as the light" (Matt 17:2). But we would be mistaken if we think it was all about Jesus. It was not. The vision aimed at transforming Jesus' disciples.

Matthew stresses their participation. Jesus selected the three leading apostles Peter, James and John to accompany him to the top of the mountain. To them God's voice is addressed saying: "This is my Son, whom I love; with him I am well pleased. Listen to him!" (Matt 17:1.5). For the vision on Mount Tabor was a 'handing on ceremony'. Jesus was handing on his mission of transforming the world and handing on his authority to the apostles. This is strongly confirmed by the appearance of Moses and Elijah (Matt 17:3–4). Any Jew in Jesus' time would have grasped their significance.

Moses himself could not conquer the promised land. Before his death, on top of a high mountain, he handed over to Joshua. "Be strong and courageous," Moses told him. "You must go with this people into the land that the Lord swore to their ancestors to give them. . . The Lord himself goes before you and will be with you; he will never leave you nor forsake you. Do not be afraid; do not be discouraged" (Deut 31:7–8).

In a similar way the prophet Elijah handed on his task and power to his disciple Elisha. When Elijah announced his departure from this earth, Elisha asked: "Let me inherit a double portion of your spirit." "You have asked a difficult thing," Elijah replied. "Yet if you see me when I am taken from you, it will be yours—otherwise not." Then a chariot of fire and horses of fire appeared and lifted Elijah up to heaven in a whirlwind. Elisha witnessed it and found that Elijah had left his cloak. Elijah picked it up. And wearing Elijah's cloak Elisha could now act as a full-fledged prophet who could act with power as his master had done (2 Kgs 2:8–15).

And here we have the full reassuring message of Jesus' transfiguration. Yes, Jesus will depart. He will be taken up to heaven. But he has handed on the continuation of his mission to the apostles and their successors. He also conferred on them his own spiritual authority. They will confront new challenges not foreseen in Jesus' lifetime. They will expand to new territory as Joshua did. They will, in unexpected novel circumstances, provide guidance to people as Elisha did.

In other words: Jesus wants ministers in the Church to courageously design and execute the updating of 'doctrines' and practices required for our present world. He promises his Spirit will guide them and give them the strength to implement any necessary reforms.

QUESTIONS

1. What is your own view in all this? Do you believe that being faithful to Sacred Tradition means holding on to the way things were in the past? Or do you agree that, on the contrary, Sacred Tradition which goes back to Jesus himself, implies the authority of church leaders to deal with new challenges and walk new paths?

2. Have you been sufficiently aware of how Jesus foresaw the need of adaptations in future times?

3. The final question: are you prepared to act? Do you have the courage to listen to Jesus' Spirit speaking in our day and age, and pursue responsible reforms?

Overview

THIS SECTION DOES NOT contain a complete systematic presentation of the contents of the Chapters. I just portray highlights. We want to reform the exercise of authority in the Church. If so, what are the implications for various ministers?

THE POPE AND BISHOPS' CONFERENCES

Some general principles should be incorporated in Church law and practice.

- The ban against the ordination of women should be lifted (Ch. 9). As a first step women should be ordained deacons (Ch. 23).

- Ministers are subject to secular law (Ch. 16). They are accountable to the community for their role in institutional management (Ch. 20).

- The Church should allow regional variation in the implementation of reforms (Ch. 26).

- Ministers should be open to the Spirit (Ch. 22). Theologians should enjoy freedom of research and expression (Ch. 10). Close attention should be given to the believers' 'sense of faith' (Ch. 13) and the voice of prophecy (Ch. 11).

- Our Christian 'liberation from law' should not be impaired by the imposition of moral obligations through Church laws (Ch. 8).

THE PEOPLE OF GOD, BOTH
MEN AND WOMEN

- The educated laity manifest their own strong opinions on what is right or what is wrong in Church practice. Church leaders should give full weight to this as it may reveal the 'sense of faith', ultimate source of the Church's inerrancy (Ch. 13).

- Ordinary members of the community may exercise sacramental functions, such as hearing confessions or presiding at the Eucharist, in the absence of ordained ministers. This is on account of latent spiritual authority acquired through baptism (Ch. 14).

- Some lay members exercise a level of authority through their ministry of teaching (Ch. 10) or prophecy (Ch. 11).

- The faithful should have an active part in decisions taken that affect the community. This can be achieved mainly through diocesan and parish pastoral councils (Ch. 12).

PRIESTS

- A priest's pastoral ministry should be people oriented. Members of the parish should be visited in their homes (Ch. 17) or in hospital when they are ill (Ch. 6).

- Priests should give special care to people with mental health problems such as guilt, anxiety or depression (Ch. 7).

- The Sunday sermon should not just be a pious talk. Rather it should provide real guidance on the integration of faith in our sophisticated secular world (Ch. 21).

- Priests should remain in touch with Catholics holding extreme views, ensuring they will not be totally isolated (Ch. 24).

BISHOPS

- Bishops should minimise the display of hierarchical pomp inherited from the past (Ch. 18).
- Bishops should not claim for themselves a level of superior dignity (Ch. 15).
- Bishops should make sure diocesan finances benefit the ministry rather than display episcopal splendor (Ch. 19).

TERMS EXPLAINED

- 'Apostles', 'heralds' (Ch. 2)
- 'Binding or loosening' (Ch. 4)
- 'Ecclesia', 'church' (Ch. 12)
- 'Kingdom of Heaven' (Ch. 2)
- 'Power of the keys' (Ch. 3)
- 'Sense of faith' (Ch. 13)

Publications by John Wijngaards

1963 *The Formulas of the Deuteronomic Creed*, **Brill, Leiden, the Netherlands.**

1965 *Vazal van Jahweh*, **Bosch & Keunig, Baarn, the Netherlands.**

1969 *The Dramatization of Salvific History in the Deuteronomic Schools*, **Brill, Leiden, the Netherlands.**

   What we can learn from secular efficiency, **St Paul Publications, New Delhi, India.**

1970 *Background to the Gospels*, **St Paul Publications, New Delhi, India.**

1971 *God's Word to Israel*, **Theological Publications, Ranchi, India.**

1973 *Deuteronomium uit de grondtekst vertaald en uitgelegd*, **Romen & Zonen, Roermond, the Netherlands.**

   Reading God's Word to others, **Asian Trading Corporation, Bangalore, India.**

1976 *Mukti Margamu*, **Amruthavani, Secunderabad, India.**

1977 *Did Christ rule out women priests?*, **McCrimmons, Great Wakering, UK.**

1978 *Brathuku Baata*, **Amruthavani, Secunderabad, India.**

   Communicating the Word of God, **McCrimmons, Great Wakering.**

1981 *Experiencing Jesus*, **Ave Maria Press, Notre Dame Indiana.**

1985 *Inheriting the Master's Cloak*, **Ave Maria Press, Notre Dame Indiana.**

1986 *The Gospel of John and his Letters*, **Michael Glazier, Wilmington DE.**

1987   *The Spirit in John*, **Michael Glazier, Wilmington DE.**

        The Seven Circles of Prayer, **McCrimmon, Great Wakering, UK.**

        Jesus for Ever. Fact & Faith, **Catholic Truth Society, London.**

1988   *God within us*, **Collins, London.**

1990   *My Galilee, My People*, **Paulist Press, Mahwah NJ.**

        For the sake of his people, **McCrimmons, Great Wakering, UK.**

1991   *Together in My Name*, **Paulist Press, Mahwah NJ.**

1992   *I have no Favourites*, **Paulist Press, Mahwah NJ.**

1995   *How to make sense of God*, **Sheed & Ward, Kansas, Missouri.**

1999   *www.womenpriests.org*, **online archive on the ordination of women.**

2001   *The Ordination of Women in the Catholic Church*, **Darton, Longman & Todd, London.**

2002   *No Women in Holy Orders? The Ancient Women Deacons*, **Canterbury Press, London.**

2007   **Major expansion of** *www.womenpriests.org*.

2011   *Amrutha. What the Pope's man found out about the law of nature*, **Author House Publications, Bloomington IN.**

2012   *www.churchauthority.org*, **website on church governance.**

2016   *www.thebodyissacred.org*, **website on the ethics of sexuality.**

2020   *What they don't teach you in Catholic College. Women in the priesthood and the mind of Christ*, **Acadian House Publishing, Lafayette Louisiana.**

2021   *Ten Commandments for Church Reform: Memoirs of a Catholic Priest*, **Acadian House Publishing, Lafayette Louisiana.**

Bibliography

Aquinas, Thomas. *Summa Theologica (1265–74)*. Einsiedeln, Switserland: Benzington Brothers, 1485; English translation. Project Gutenberg, 1920.

Benson, Robert Louis. *Bishop-Elect: A Study in Medieval Ecclesiastical Office*. Princeton Legacy Library 2117. Princeton, NJ: Princeton University Press, 2015.

Bermejo, Luis. *Infallibility on Trial: Church, Conciliarity and Communion*. Westminster, MD: Christian Classics, 1992.

Berry, Jason. *Render unto Rome: The Secret Life of Money in the Catholic Church*. New York: Crown, 2011.

Bianchi, Eugene C., and Rosemary Radford Ruether, eds. *A Democratic Catholic Church*. New York: Crossroad, 1992.

Boff, Leonardo. *Church, Charism and Power (English Translation)*. New York: Crossroad, 1985.

Canon Law Society. *The Code of Canon Law*. London: Collins, 1983.

Chapman, Mark, and Vladimir Latinovic. *Changing the Church: Transformations of Christian Belief, Practice, and Life*. Springer: Palgrave Macmillan, 2020.

Chirico, Peter. *Infallibility: The Crossroads of Doctrine*. Wilmington: Glazier, 1983.

Clark, William, and Daniel Gast, eds. *Collaborative Parish Leadership: Contexts, Models, Theology*. Lanham, MD: Lexington, 2017.

Collins, Paul, *Papal Power: A Proposal for Change in Catholicism's Third Millennium*. London: HarperCollins, 1997.

———. *Upon This Rock: The Popes and Their Changing Role*. Melbourne, Aust.: Melbourne University Press, 2000.

Confalonieri, Luca Badini. *Democracy in the Christian Church: An Historical, Theological and Political Case*. London: Black, 2012.

Congar, Yves. *Lay People in the Church: A Study for a Theology of the Laity*. London: Geoffrey Chapman, 1957.

Connolly, Terence, and John Hunt. *The Responsibility of Dissent: The Church and Academic Freedom*. London: Sheed & Ward, 1970.

Curran, Charles, and Robert Hunt. *Dissent in and for the Church: Theologians and Humane Vitae*. Sheed & Ward, 1970.

Curran, Charles. *Faithful dissent*. New York: Sheed and Ward, 1986.

135

Daurelle, Claire. "My Vocation." In *Dans les Églises, des Femmes aussi sont ministères*, 48–52. Paris: 1996.

Finucane, Daniel. *Sensus Fidelium: The Use of a Concept in the Post-Vatican II Era*. Eugene, OR: Wipf & Stock, 2016.

Flannery, Austin, ed. *Vatican Council II*. Northport, NY: Costello, 1988.

Fransen, Piet, and Leonard Swidler, eds. *Authority in the Church and the Schillebeeckx Case*. New York: Crossroad, 1982.

Friedberg, Aemilius, ed. *Corpus Juris Canonici*. Leipzig: Tauchnitz 1879–81; reprint Graz 1955.

Granfield, Patrick. *The Limits of the Papacy: Authority and Autonomy in the Church*. New York: Crossroad, 1990.

Haag, Herbert. *Clergy & Laity. Did Jesus want a Two-Tier Church?* London: Burns & Oates, 1998.

Hahnenberg, Edward. *Theology for Ministry: An Introduction for Lay Ministers*. Collegeville, MN: Liturgical, 2014.

Hertling, Ludwig. *Communio: Church and Papacy in Early Christianity*. Chicago: Loyola University Press, 1972.

Hinze, Bradford, and Peter Phan. *Learning from All the Faithful: A Contemporary Theology of the Sensus Fidei*. Eugene, OR: Wipf & Stock, 2016.

Hoose, Bernard, ed. *Authority in the Roman Catholic Church. Theory & Practice*. Farnham, UK: Ashgate, 2002.

International Theological Commission. *Sensus Fidei in the Life of the Church*. London: Catholic Truth Society, 2014.

John Paul II, Pope. *Ordinatio Sacerdotalis*. Rome: Congregation for Doctrine, 22 May 1994.

Küng, Hans, and Leonard Swidler, eds. *The Church in Anguish: Has the Vatican Betrayed Vatican II?* New York: Harper & Row, 1986.

Küng, Hans. *Infallible? An Unresolved Inquiry*. London: SCM, 1994.

Lakeland, Paul. *A Council That Will Never End: Lumen Gentium and the Church Today*. Collegeville, MN: Liturgical Press, 2013.

———. *Catholicism at the Crossroads. How the Laity can Save the Church*. New York: Continuum, 2007.

———. *The Liberation of the Laity: In Search of an Accountable Church*. New York: Continuum, 2004.

Last, Richard. *The Pauline Church and the Corinthian Ekklēsia: Greco-Roman Associations in Comparative Context*. Cambridge University Press, 2016.

Lee, Dorothy A. *The Ministry of Women in the New Testament: Reclaiming the Biblical Vision for Church Leadership*. Ada, MI: Baker Academic, 2021.

Luciani, Rafael. *Synodality: A New Way of Proceeding in the Church*. New York: Paulist, 2022.

Mannion, Gerard, ed. *Readings in Church Authority*. Farnham, UK: Ashgate, 2003.

Mannion, Gerard, et al., eds. *Readings in Church Authority: Gifts and Challenges for Contemporary Catholicism*. Abingdon: Routledge, 2017.

Maxwell, John Francis. "The Development of Catholic Doctrine Concerning Slavery." *World Jurist* 11 (1969–70) 306–7.

Miller, Virginia, et al., eds. *Leaning into the Spirit: Ecumenical Perspectives on Discernment and Decision-Making in the Church*. Cham Switzerland: Palgrave Macmillan, 2019.

Mobbs, Frank. *Beyond its Authority: The Magisterium and Matters of Natural Law*. Alexandria NSW: E. J. Dwyer, 1997.

Newman, John Henry. *On Consulting the Laity in Matters of Doctrine*. Edited by John Coulson. London: Collins, 1961.

O'Hanlon, Gerr., *The Quiet Revolution of Pope Francis: A Synodal Catholic Church in Ireland?* Dublin: Irish Messenger Publications, 2021.

Oakley, Francis, and Bruce Russett, eds. *Governance, Accountability and the Future of the Catholic Church*. Yale University, 2003.

Paul VI, Pope. *Inter Insigniores*. Rome: Congregation of the Faith, 15 October 1976.

Pius XII, Pope. *Humani Generis*. Rome: Congregation for Doctrine, 12 August 1950.

Prüller-Jagenteufel, Gunter, et al., eds. *Towards Just Gender Relations. Rethinking the Role of Women in Church and Society*. Göttingen: Vandenhoeck & Ruprecht, 2019.

Ratzinger, Josef. "The Pastoral Implications of Episcopal Collegiality." *Concilium* 1965.

Reese, Thomas J., ed. *Episcopal Conferences: Historical, Canonical and Theological Studies*. Georgetown University Press, 1989.

Schillebeeckx, Edward. *Ministry: Leadership in the Community of Jesus Christ*. New York: Crossroad, 1981.

———. *The Church with a Human Face: A New and Expanded Theology of Ministry*. New York: Crossroad, 1990.

Seidler, John. *Conflict and Change in the Catholic church*. Rutgers University Press, 1989.

Seidler, John, and Katherine Meyer. *Conflict and Change in the Catholic Church*. Rutgers University Press, 1989.

Shannon, James Patrick, *The Reluctant Dissenter*. New York: Crossroad, 1998.

Sullivan, Francis. *Magisterium: Teaching Authority in the Catholic Church*. Dublin: Gill and Macmillan, 1983.

Swidler, Leonard, and Herbert O'Brien, eds. *A Catholic Bill of Rights*. Kansas City: Sheed and Ward, 1988.

Vaillancourt, Jean-Guy. *Papal Power. A Study of Vatican Control over Lay Catholic Elites*. Berkeley: University of California, 1980.

Van Lierde, Peter Canisius. *The Holy See at Work: How the Catholic Church is Governed*. London: Hale, 1962.

Wijngaards John. "God and Our New Selves." *Religioni e Sette del Mondo* 4 (1998) 172–93.

———. *The Gospel of John and His Letters*. Wilmington, DL: Michael Glazier, 1986.

——. The Ordination of Women in the Catholic Church. *Unmasking a Cuckoo's Egg Tradition*. London: Darton, Longman & Todd, 2001.

——. *Ten Commandments for Church Reform*, Lafayette: Acadian, 2021.

——. *Women Deacons in the Early Church*. New York: Herder & Herder Crossroad, 2006.

Wills, Garry. *Papal sin. The Structures of Deceit*. London: Darton Longman & Todd, 2000.